# After the Tears

RECLAIMING THE
PERSONAL
LOSSES OF
CHILDHOOD

JANE MIDDELTON-MOZ & LORIE DWINELL

Published by Health Communications, Inc.
Enterprise Center
3201 S.W. 15th Street
Deerfield Beach, FL 33442

ISBN 0-932194-36-2

Cover Illustration and Design by Reta Kaufman

# Dedications

Jane Middelton-Moz, dedicates this book to:

> My husband, Rudolph Moz, for being my best friend, my supporter, a consistent mentor who has taught me so much of the human mind and heart.

> My children, Shawn, Jason, Damien, Forrest and Melinda, for sharing with me your uniquely wonderful selves and love.

> My brother, Alex E. Ward, for always being there.

Lorie Dwinell dedicates this book to:

> My mother, Betty Dwinell Archer, to whom I am ever grateful for the good job you did not only in raising us but in staying the course and working through your own early life pain so that we could become best friends.

> My brothers, Bill and David Dwinell. We are in this together.

> My best friends, Wynn Bloch, Claudia Black, and Jane Middelton-Moz from whom I have learned unconditional love.

We both dedicate this book to our clients and the Adult Children whom we have known who have shared so much and taught us all we know, and the Adult Children who we are.

# Acknowledgments

The authors would like to acknowledge the tremendous support of many individuals during the germination and writing of *After The Tears:*

Alex Barker, Jo Kelly, Nanci Presley-Holley, and Madeline Johnson for the gifts of their creative talents.

Claudia Black, a native Washingtonian and personal friend, for her professional contributions.

Wynn Bloch, Susan Harris, Gina Delmastro and Kathy Munson for their consistent support and feedback through their work as "roving therapists" at our workshops over the past seven years.

Auriel Clare, Wynn Bloch, and Dave Zeigen for their impeccable English and excellent grammar in the editing of *After The Tears.*

Glenda Downs, for her patience and work on the word processor.

Carol Hobart, a talented, creative, fine artist who has illustrated *After The Tears.*

Rudolph I. Moz, for his consistent help, advice, and encouragement.

Darlene Thomas, who has patiently and diligently worked on the word processor and has served as the major support staff for our workshops over the past seven years.

The Staff and Board of Seattle Mental Health Institute for their consistent support, feedback, and the use of the facility over the last seven years.

*The U.S. Journal* for affording us the opportunity to be introduced to a wide range of other professional people who have increased our knowledge and validated our work in the field.

A special thanks to our clients and the participants in our workshops without whose personal knowledge and sharing as Adult Children, this book would have never been possible.

# Table of Contents

# Introduction

Why did we write this book? Well, that's a good question. Probably an honest answer is that Jane Middelton-Moz had a burning desire to share the depth and breadth of what she knows about grief resolution for individuals affected by parental alcoholism, and invited me along for the "write." We have been "gestating" this book for about seven years and have been seriously thinking about what we wanted to convey for the past two years. Of the two of us, Jane is the "real" author, *i.e.*, the one who willingly takes pen in hand to share what she knows. I, on the other hand, am the "verbal historian," the public speaker, the metaphor-maker who must be coaxed to get my part down on paper. Here is the final product of this, our initial collaboration.

When we began, we took on the ambitious project of wanting to write a book which would encompass *all* of the areas which we felt were important for work with Adult Children and the helping professionals who work with ACoAs. Such a book would address topics as diverse as object choice, gender identification, self-esteem, domestic violence, sexual abuse, coping skill repertoires, eating disorders, addictions, and spirituality. We found, however, that the longer we worked on the book the more we moved away from an all-encompassing "textbook" full of professional jargon, and more and more in the direction of a book which we hope will satisfy the needs of both Adult Children and helping professionals in making sense of the Adult-Child Syndrome and the grief resolution process which is integral to recovery. Although we have tried to keep professional jargon to a minimum, there are some technical terms in the text. When we have used a technical term, we have tried to juxtapose it with a definition to help make sense of it.

Jane Middelton-Moz and I are, first and foremost, clinicians, and it is our hope that this book will serve as both a cognitive map and as a beacon to light the way in the journey towards health and wholeness, not only for the many Adult Children with whom we have worked, but also for the many others who are trying to reconnect their feelings with repressed memories of the past. Although our specific audience is Adult Children who were raised in alcoholic homes, this book could also have been entitled *Adult Children of Dysfunctional Families*, for any family in which there is a major trauma which is denied rather than discussed and worked through, will produce the same syndrome or variations on the same theme.

Many of the individuals for whom this book was written are also recovering from an array of other disorders symptomatic of both the genetic and emotional liabilities of early childhood experiences in alcoholic families. Numbered among you are recovering alcoholics/addicts, compulsive spenders/gamblers, sexual or relationship addicts, workaholics, compulsive overeaters, etc. We salute you in your recovery and hope that this book will assist you on the next leg of your journey. Jane Middelton-Moz and I are both long-term optimists who believe that human beings are open systems shaped by, but not determined by, their pasts.

— Lorie Dwinell, A.C.S.W.

*This poem was originally written for and dedicated to Lorie Dwinell in 1980.*

### Juggler In A Mirror

*From that place inside of me*
*That learning, yearning, writer in me*
*I saw by touch, not from sight*
*A woman who passed my way in life*
*Who shared a person I recognized*
*As standing like myself.*

*I watched her juggle as she stood*
*Words and feelings made of wood*
*Sticks that talked of competence*
*Of strength and will and confidence*
*And four or five marked child and home*
*And one marked guilt that cracked and hit*
*The others as they flew.*

*She tossed up two marked love and care*
*That hung above her in the air*
*And one marked trust beneath the two*
*That stopped the lower sticks marked you*
*From soaring in the sky.*

*So skillfully she juggled life*
*That I would not have recognized*
*The perspiration in her face*
*That drew me to her side*
*If not for one large purple stick*
*That dropped behind her with a click*
*And called its name out loud and clear*
*The one she could not juggle fear.*

*I could not watch, it hurt too much*
*And I thought between the two of us*
*That we could balance all some way*
*And pay the price survivors pay*
*Who stand alone in streets and crowds*
*Destined to juggle sticks.*

*Perhaps we both could recognize*
*That none that we had met in life*
*Had taught us how to juggle sticks.*
*They had passed them on to us with doubt*
*With tears that never made it from the inside out*
*They had dropped them all, save two or three*
*The sticks marked child and family.*

by Jane Middelton (Moz)
from Juggler In A Mirror (1980)

## Chapter One

# Self-Sufficient
# In An Insufficient Way

"The alley is dark and cold. I'm sitting about halfway down it on a couple of shabby empty suitcases. I'm wearing a dark blue coat that I've pulled tightly around me to keep warm, but it doesn't seem to help. I know I'm alone in the world, and I also know that I've finally gone totally crazy. The only thing that I have that's mine is my diploma from medical school. I'm holding it in both hands, and I'm almost crumpling it, I'm holding it so tight. Then a figure floats up the alley toward me — a man. At first I can't make out who it is, but then, as he gets closer I recognize him. It's the Dean of the medical school I attended. He looms up in front of me and grabs for my diploma and it seems to slip out of my hands as it it didn't really exist. He's furious, yelling at me, 'You didn't earn this! You don't deserve this! Who do you think you are?' His voice seems to be all around me as it booms down the alley. And then I wake up." Beth pauses for a minute and adds, "I'm sorry. You must hear a million stupid dreams," thereby totally discounting the story she has just related.

Beth was an exceptionally competent professional woman. She graduated at the top of her high school class and earned a scholarship to undergraduate school. She continued her academic success in college, not only graduating with top honors, but also winning a scholarship to medical school. After completing her medical training, she moved to a small town in the East where she developed a highly successful practice. She entered therapy at the age of 35 after her second divorce because, as she said, "The bottom is falling out of my life." She felt that nothing was real, that her whole life had been a lie. She worried about everything — her career, her divorce, her past, the process of therapy, and whether her therapist felt that she was nothing more than a "whining child." During one of her therapy sessions, she reported her repetitive dream which for her had become a metaphor of her life.

On the surface, Richard's life seemed quite different from Beth's. Richard was court-referred to alcoholism treatment after his second drunk driving charge. His early life history indicated that he had a great deal of difficulty in school, although his teachers felt that "he was a smart kid who just didn't pay attention." He dropped out of school at 16 and later earned his GED Certificate at the age of 25. He felt that the only two accomplishments in his entire life had been his GED and a diploma he received from an alcohol treatment facility prior to his beginning therapy. After his first year of sobriety he told his therapist, "I'm sober and I'm really proud of it. One day at a time hasn't been easy. I've worked hard at it, but deep down inside I feel that I'll screw up my life again, maybe this time not through drinking, but through something else. I've always been a jerk. I feel like I'm not doing this right either. It's not your fault, you're a good therapist, but I've just never quite done it right. In AA they would tell me that I'm sitting on the pity pot. Maybe that's true, but it's just that things never work out for me."

Beth and Richard appear to be very different individuals with quite different paths and life experiences. Yet, individual therapy and in their therapy group, they found that they shared a common history — both had similar feelings and a similar experience of the world — and both had alcoholic parents. It wasn't that both had grown up in the same city and had gone to the same high school, but that both had felt lonely, and both had never felt quite as good as their classmates. Despite her popularity and many friendships, Beth felt that she was never very close to anyone. Richard envied those who were always surrounded by other people because he felt he could never connect and make friends. He was extremely "shy." Both grew up in middle-class suburban neighborhoods with lots of kids close by, but each felt estranged and without friends.

Beth and Richard both grew up with alcoholic parents, but until therapy, each had little or no understanding of how parental alcoholism had affected their lives and development. Beth and Richard each talked about traumatic events from childhood as if they were talking about somone else's life, showing little feeling about or for the children they used to be. Both were depressed and were suffering from unresolved or delayed grief.

It would be fair to ask, "grieve for what?" Why in these two individuals was grief delayed or unresolved, and what accounts for the similarities in how both Beth and Richard have apparently detached from the trauma they experienced in the alcoholic families in which they were reared?

Growing up in an alcoholic home has been characterized as similar in stress to being in the Nazi Concentration Camps of World War II. (Vaillant, 1983). One Adult Child of an alcoholic described his early life experience in the following way, "I often felt in growing up with my alcoholic father that I was living with an atomic bomb in the basement and at any time it would go off without warning. Living with my co-dependent mother was like living with another atomic bomb, only this one was in the attic."

This young man felt that the stress of the unpredictability and capriciousness of his alcoholic father was equally matched by the stress of his co-dependent mother's hyper-reactivity when the binge drinking occurred.

Alcoholism is like living with "an air raid a day."

Under these conditions, chronic stress becomes normal. In order to protect the ego from the disintegration which would result from assaulting it regularly with that magnitude of trauma, individuals learn to adapt with massive denial and repression. Living with both the constant unpredictability of the alcoholic parent and the detachment/derangement of the co-dependent parent, who is pre-empted by the stress, is difficult enough for an adult who has a fully developed defense system. A child will have to employ massive amounts of energy merely to survive. This puts the normal development process on hold; there is no energy left to invest in development. The end result is a child who often feels thirty years old at five and five years old at thirty.

### The Maddening New Year's Eve Party
*(this poem was written by an eight-year-old child)*

Twas the night before New Year's

When all through the house

Many creatures were stirring

Including a mouse.

The grown-ups were sipping their cocktails with care

In hopes that more bourbon would soon be there.

A man was dressed as a green alligator

And a woman's dress was torn in the seater.

A drunk man was running all around

He started down stairs, but instead he fell down.

For supper they had fried frog legs and snails

And a man got so nervous he was biting his nails.

*By Alexandra*

The chronic trauma of living in any family where the focus is on an addiction, rather than on the needs of developing children, places at least three burdens on these youngsters as they grow up: First, the repeated experience of the trauma itself; second, the effects of the trauma on personality development; and last, the need to re-experience the original trauma in order to integrate it and work it through. The effects on personality development and the process of integration will be discussed in subsequent chapters. The remainder of this chapter will focus on the children's reactions to the trauma experienced as a result of parental alcoholism.

## The Burden of Traumatic Experiences

Sandler (1967) describes trauma as any experience that within a short period of time presents the mind with a stimulus too powerful to be assimilated or mastered in a normal way. The stimulus (internal or external) results in the child experiencing a state of helplessness. In discussing the effect of a traumatic experience on a child, we will return to a traumatic event related by Beth in individual therapy.

Beth described this experience during her fifth month of therapy. Although the event was highly stressful, she talked about it with apparent detachment. She started by talking about a problem she had experienced in both of her marriages. She said that she would become anxious and panic any time her husband would be late coming home or on occasions when he had to leave the house after dark. If she left the house in the evening, she felt fine, experiencing neither panic nor anxiety. Her "attacks" would occur only if she were left alone in the house. All of her attempts to occupy herself or soothe herself when alone had failed miserably. She would go to bed and fantasize that her husband was with her or she would extract elaborate assurances and promises from him that he would be home at a designated time, none of which allayed her fears. When alone, she was hyper-sensitive to any noise she heard or thought she heard, and her "startle reaction" would be accompanied by sweats, "the jitters," stomach aches, and constant focusing on food.

When asked if she experienced similar panic after dark now that she was separated from her husband and living on her own, she answered, "Well, no, but then there is no one to be jealous of now. I've been told so often that it was jealousy, but," she said with a puzzled look, "I'm really not the jealous type and never was prior to marriage. Why would marriage, just the fact of marriage, do that to me?"

The therapist answered Beth's question with a question: "Do you recall being afraid of the dark at any time when you were a child?" Beth could not recall being afraid of the dark when she was young, but then remembered a "scarey" time that had happened when she was about eight years old. It was Saturday. There had been a terrible storm the night before and the storm had increased during the day. It was spring and the river that separated her house from the town had flooded and washed out the surrounding roads for miles. The power was out and the telephone lines were down. Her father hadn't been able to get home. She said that her mother first started acting nervous and then angry. She had seen her mother like that at other times when she could not get her drinks.

Beth laughed as she said that her father would sometimes pour her mother's liquor down the sink, and then her parents would have terrible fights about it. Even at the young age of eight, she realized that it wasn't her father being stuck in town that bothered her mom, but that he usually brought liquor home on Friday nights and that he couldn't because of the storm. Her father was not able to get home for almost four days and the rest of the family couldn't get to town. She remembered many instances of her mother's rage and panic during those four days, of which she bore most of the brunt. She told stories of trying to make food for herself and her brothers out of flour and water and was proud of the "crackers" she had created. Then she spoke of her mother's crazy behavior after the second day, laughing as she told of her mother trying to hit bugs that weren't there. Beth did not realize until she was in medical school that her mother had been having D.T.'s and so must have been alcoholic. She also felt guilty at not taking better care of her and felt badly that she had not had sufficient knowledge at the time to know what to do.

When one imagines what must have been experienced by that eight-year-old child, not only left with the responsibility of younger children housebound by a storm, but also with the care of a mother in delirium tremens, it seems terrifying. Yet, Beth showed little empathy for the child. She was only critical because she hadn't done better. She denied any anger at being placed in such a helpless position at such a young age. As other memories surfaced, it was obvious that she had had similar experiences when even younger. Instead, panic and terror experienced as a child did not show itself until as a grown woman she was left alone after dark. Like so many children raised in alcoholic homes, Beth had felt and acted thirty at the age of eight, and now she was acting eight at the age of thirty.

In a traumatic situation such as the one just described, a child becomes flooded and overwhelmed by the emotions felt. The response is to first freeze in a helpless state of anxiety and then to experience a sensation of numbness, feeling like someone else is watching the event — a type of unreality. If the child remained flooded in that helpless state, he/she could not continue to be functional or sane. Instead, to buffer the impact of the emotional flooding, the child's ego creates an elaborate barrier of defense mechanisms to protect itself from the experience. If a soldier fighting on a battlefield really experiences the sights and sounds around him, realizes that his friend has died next to him, or allows the possibility that he could die to enter his consciousness, he could not survive physically or mentally; neither can a child living through the chaotic and frightening experiences that often occur in an alcoholic family.

In a healthy environment, a child has parents who function as that emotional "buffer." They stand between the child and the trauma, being what Mahler (1968) refers to as "the protective shield." But what if, as Beth experienced, the parents are not only the "buffer," but also the agents inflicting the pain? A soldier can focus anger on an enemy that he can rationalize deserves his anger. For a child to consciously feel anger toward a parent, or to recognize a parent as non-protective, would be to feel even more helpless and face a trauma of far greater magnitude — *abandonment*. In order to feel safe and protected, a child develops personal resources and defenses prematurely, thereby continuing to protect a fantasy ideal of the "powerful and protective" parent. The child learns to "shut off" the experience through detachment, and with it, her or his own developmental process.

Many different mechanisms can be used to defend an ego under emotional attack: *Repression* buries the incident as well as the emotions it generated in the child's unconscious; *denial* can create the fiction that mother was only a little ill and that it wasn't "that big a thing;" *reversal* puts the child in the position of taking care of the parent rather than receiving care from the parent. The child may identify with the aggressor and believe that he/she was the cause of the incident; *through projection* the child may believe the parent to be stupid, but powerful; or the child may punish herself/himself rather than consciously feel the anger towards the parent (anger turned inward).

Sandler (1967) agrees with the findings of other researchers (Freud and Breuer, 1955) when through his own investigation he found that extended or repetitive situations of stress in a child's life might combine to create trauma to the ego even though each incident on its own might not be considered to be as traumatic as the one just discussed.

Alcoholic families live in a state of crisis which has become normalized. Perhaps the major pathogenic factor in alcoholic families is the denial of the reality of the deviant drinking and its impact on the children. For children in these families, life is lived as "rehearsal for traumatic events" (Wegscheider-Cruse, 1981). These children cannot allow themselves to feel the impact of the trauma and also maintain the ability to function with it on an ongoing basis. The survival adaption which these children develop can be likened to "chronic shock syndrome" (Cermack, 1984) with the attendant psychic numbing, restricted affect, hypervigilance, and recurrent intrusive dreams and flashbacks of earlier traumatic experiences. The home environments of these children are what Frederic Flach (1974, p. 156) calls "depressogenic." These homes lack ego support, prevent the development of *healthy* self-reliance, create hostility and block its release, promote feelings of guilt, and cause the child to feel lonely and rejected. Such an environment engenders a chronic, pervasive sense of loss which tends to be out of conscious awareness and predisposes children raised in these homes to problems with depression in adolescence and adulthood.

These "depression-prone" individuals are highly sensitized to situations of real or potential loss and abandonment and closely match Flach's (1974) description of the person predisposed to depression: "vulnerable to loss; conscientious; responsible; ambitious; competitive; self-absorbed; strongly in need of the approval and acceptance of others; dependent upon those whom he/she loves; inflexible; highly sensitive (especially to rejection); vulnerable to being controlled by others; and unaware of feelings, especially those of anger." (Flach, 1974, pp. 1-219)

Denial is the hallmark of an alcoholic family and, hence, it is no surprise that these families provide little or no support for the children to work through the pain of the absence of the parenting that would occur in a growth-fostering family context. A child is not able to discern that he or she is interacting with the illness of alcoholism or the "mirror" illness of co-dependency, rather than with a parent. Hence, the child tends to internalize blame for all that goes wrong and embarks on what can become a life-long career of hyper-responsibility, perfectionism, conflict avoidance, and caretaking. This is a misplaced attempt to save his/her alcoholic parent and to integrate the traumatic experience through cognitive and emotional mastery of it.

A paradigm developed by Burgan (1974) clarifies this internalization process and illustrates how alcoholism is often a training ground for what Seligman (1975) calls "learned helplessness." The five stick figures here represent five states of sobriety/intoxication in an alcoholic mother.

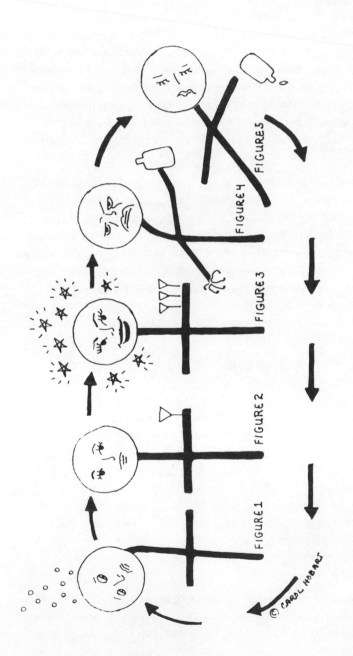

In Figure 1, the parent is nauseated, irritable, and hung-over. When her eight-year-old daughter asks for a sandwich, the mother responds, "Leave me alone! You're nothing but trouble. Can't you see I don't feel well?" A few minutes later the little girl returns still hungry and determined this time to "get it right." She asks her mother ever so carefully if she can fix herself a sandwich.

In Figure 2, her mother is warm and responsive, having drunk enough alcohol to alleviate her withdrawal symptoms. She offers to fix her daughter a sandwich and gives her a choice of peanut butter and jelly or bologna and cheese. The little girl feels really loved and thinks that she must remember just how she asked her mother for a sandwich this second time so that she will get the same loving response the next time she asks.

In Figure 3, the mother has had enough to drink to be on the rising side of a blood/alcohol curve. She is expansive and intoxicated and when her little girl comes back later to get the sandwich, the mother pulls her down on her lap, smothers her with wet, yucky kisses, and tells her that since she's the best little girl in the world she'll buy her a ten-speed bike later that afternoon. Needless to say, this is music to the little girl's ears, especially since her interactions with her mother are an emotional feast or famine, thereby exacerbating her normal needs for affection, approval, and dependency. She doesn't like the wet, yucky kisses, but the promise of a bike makes her feel loved and special.

In Figure 4, when the little girl comes running back in from play she says, "Mommy, can we go downtown to get my bike?" Unfortunately, her mother is now on the falling side of a blood/alcohol curve and is drunk, depressed, and irritable. She snarls, "Get the hell out of my face, you ugly little brat. I can't stand you." The little girl recoils, surprised, frightened, and her defense against the despair of feeling unloved and rejected by her mother is to blame herself. She decides she's stupid, ugly, clumsy, and can't do anything right. She should have been more attentive and worked harder around the house rather than being outside. Eventually she comes to believe that since she caused her parent's behavior, she should be able to change it.

In Figure 5, her mother is *passed out* — a state that a very small child confuses with "dead" until she learns that mother is "sleeping" or "drunk." The little girl in this example represses the event, learns to feel powerless, apathetic, and helpless; nothing she does makes a difference. She is also learning to be hypervigilant, noticing even the smallest shift in her mother's speech, moods, or behavior. She is "adult" in the face of an everchanging reality which constantly provokes a surplus of feelings and necessitates a surplus of denial on her part. She has no time to process and achieve emotional and cognitive mastery over the experience before the next stressful event takes place.

Many of us know children who have recovered from traumatic events with little or no lasting effects on their personality development. What makes the difference is the support available for working it through. Any trauma can be integrated if it can be talked about, "walked through," and processed. As Sandler (p. 168) points out, "What would seem to be crucial in deciding the outcome of a traumatic experience is not so much the experience itself, as the post-traumatic state of the ego strain that it engenders and the child's ability to adapt to that state."

Waelder (1967) presents an example of a child with support from his environment "working through" a traumatic situation. A little boy, six or seven, was walking through the woods with his father when his father was suddenly attacked by a stag. His father was hurt very badly and bled profusely. This is certainly a traumatic event for a young child and the little boy stood by helplessly frozen during the attack.

As weeks progressed, the little boy continued to act out the scene over and over again in his play changing its content with each new rehearsal. Finally, one day the little boy acted out the event again. This time rather than being the witness to the event and frozen in terror, the little boy became the hero who saved his father from the frightening stag. The little boy's ego won mastery of the event little by little, thus reducing its effect on his ego development because he didn't need to repress it. He had the support to remember it, feel it, and master its effects through time. This little boy had two things present for him that Children of Alcoholics often do not have — supportive parents who could verify that the event took place, and time to work it through. Because the stag wasn't part of his daily life and he wasn't dependent on its protection, he could act out his anger at it instead of turning that anger on himself. Children in alcoholic homes can't be angry at the parents they depend on for care.

### She Was My Mother Bless Her Soul

i sometimes sit

in the corner

in the dark

and recall my mother

with a brown bottle in her hand

or the sounds of clanking ice at 2 a.m.

she'd call me baby if she wanted another beer

or a slut if she hadn't had enough

she'd make me cookies on Christmas

before she'd get too drunk

many nights

she would fall asleep on the floor

i'd cover her with a blanket

and put a pillow under her head

i'd awaken in the morning

to the sounds of her

screaming

she wasn't an easy woman to please

most of the time

we didn't get along

*sometimes i miss her*

*and the loneliness*

by Jane Middelton (Moz)
from Juggler In a Mirror (1980)

Children in alcoholic families usually do successfully develop their own internal "buffer" to traumatic events. Events that render them helpless at five almost seem to be taken as expected occurrences at age eleven. A little boy, who may have frozen in a state of helplessness at age four while witnessing his father in an alcoholic rage attacking his mother, may, at age eight, step in the middle and take the brunt of the attack himself. Unlike the little boy in Waelder's (1967) example who took on the stag in a fantasy play, Children of Alcoholics become so internally defended that they take on the "enemy" in real life. As Anna Freud stated (1967), "In the upbringing of children where frustration, criticism, and punishment are concerned, it is well known that the individual child tends to adapt to the level of parental handling and reacts traumatically only to the unexpected or the unfamiliar. A harsh scolding or slaps by a habitually tolerant parent may have a devastating *'traumatic'* effect on a child while the same treatment is assimilated in a much less dramatic manner by the children of harsh and exacting parents." The price of this, however, is that the massive amounts of energy used in defensive adaption are then not available for use in the often difficult process of normal psychological development.

To illustrate this, we'll return to the history of Richard, with whom we began this chapter. Richard said that he had a great deal of difficulty in school even though his school records showed that he was a bright child with no indication of perceptual difficulties. Many times it was recorded in the school's files that "Richard just didn't pay attention."

During therapy, Richard's account of his family experience made apparent the effects of trauma on the development of his image of himself and on his ability to pay attention in school. It was also apparent that early in his life he had constructed his own "buffer" of defenses against the trauma. This "buffer" was now causing difficulties in his life.

Unlike Beth, Richard's role in the family was not one of taking care of the family or being a child who put energy into achievement and perfectionism at an early age. Richard recalled many childhood experiences of witnessing the abusive rage of his alcoholic father that was usually directed at his mother. He reported hiding in his room and trying to make the noise go away while his older sister (much like Beth) attempted to "reason" with her parents. Richard, unlike Beth, was not only overstimulated, but due to his sister's partial "buffering," had no active role in attempting mastery of the traumatic events in his family.

Fantasize for a moment: Take your homework assignment to a video arcade with the hope of studying and perhaps even writing a report while there. Imagine trying to shut out the flashing lights and the high-pitched beeps. Richard, like anyone who might attempt to study at a video arcade, found himself constantly overstimulated both externally by what was happening in his family and internally by his feelings about it. As he got older, he learned to partially block out the external stimuli, but he had less success in controlling his constant internal responses to the traumatic episodes in his family. He was a compulsive reader as a late adolescent and young adult. He would come to each therapy session with a book in hand much as someone would wear a particular type of clothing or a badge. Usually the theme of the books was *man's dilemma* or the *meaning of life*. Like so many Children of Alcoholics, Richard consistently tried to achieve mastery through cognitive understanding. It was as if Richard was communicating through the symbol of the books he carried: "Perhaps if I can find meaning in this book, suffering too will have meaning; perhaps if someone in this novel shares my experience, then I will have a witness to the fact that I too exist; or perhaps if I carry a book I'll be like those other smart kids in school."

Richard said that many times as an adolescent, he didn't care much about what was happening at home and he often thought his sister was stupid for putting so much energy into taking care of people who obviously didn't want to be taken care of. He would say at other times that "I am just like my old man," adding, "Yeah, all the men in my family are alcoholics." He would laugh when he talked of how stupid he thought he was and how much he had messed up his life, feeling that it was somehow his *Karma*. Often, he could no longer make eye contact and would blankly stare into space. It was obvious that Richard had "identified with the aggressor" early in his life, perhaps to feel less helpless in a situation he could not control. He used massive amounts of energy denying his feelings and the effects that his early life history had on him. Like so many Children of Alcoholics he was plagued by constant guilt, but the only feeling he expressed was anger; he couldn't feel the tears.

Both of us have worked with hundreds of children from alcoholic families in our clinical practices and agree with Bettelheim's observations on the possible emotional outcomes for survivors of chronic trauma. There are probably three outcomes. First, there are those individuals who literally succumb to the destructive influences of their childhoods through suicide, insanity, or through being incarcerated for much of their lives. These people are not able to establish adequate defenses for survival, remain overwhelmed, or turn the energy of the stimulus against themselves. For whatever reason, they are unable to feel hopeful about themselves or move beyond their self-defeating behaviors.

Second, there are those individuals who use massive amounts of denial, repression, projection, and other defenses to function but do so in a restrictive way. They have learned well how to "survive," but have difficulty "living" their lives. They often find themselves in environments which, over and over again, emotionally replicate the environments of their childhood — environments which demand the defenses they have learned to exist behind, while attempting to achieve mastery of their pain. They have great difficulty when the demands of their environments exceed their ability to "defend" or to integrate more trauma.

Third, and this is the goal toward which we can all move, there are those who are able to re-experience the pain of the original trauma and work it through. Such working through is the essence of the grief work process and entails beginning to talk with one other person with whom one has established trust about how it was and how one wishes it could have been.

Chapter Two

# The Gift
# That Goes On Giving

Joan came into therapy after several months of severe depression. Prior to entering treatment, she had made one suicide attempt and had thought daily about ending her life. While relating her history, she shared extremely painful memories with little or no emotion. Both of her parents had been raised in alcoholic homes. During the course of therapy, Joan often expressed more grief over her parents' childhood losses than over her own. Joan's mother had longed to be a dancer but her own father's alcoholism had made it impossible for her to take lessons. From early childhood on, Joan's room had been decorated with posters, figurines, lamps, and wallpaper of famous ballerinas in graceful poses. At age four or five, when other children were out playing games, Joan dutifully practiced hour upon hour under her mother's watchful eye in order to someday fulfill her mother's unfulfilled dreams.

But Joan remembered feeling that she was never quite good enough. Her mother was never completely happy with her even when Joan won a full scholarship to college for her ability to dance. However, Joan kept working to gain her mother's acceptance and, most of all, her love. By age twenty-one, Joan had made her mark and was appearing as a dancer on stages all over the country. She was the object of much adoration and fanfare, and her mother was there to see her perform — when she was not too drunk. In spite of all of the honors and applause, Joan felt a deep sense of loneliness as well as a nagging feeling that the applause didn't belong to her. In her late twenties, she fell on stage and severely tore the muscles in both legs. She was told it would be some time before she would be able to dance again. To her surprise, Joan first experienced a slight feeling of relief followed, almost immediately, by frightening suicidal thoughts.

In therapy, Joan would draw her memories and feelings because it was so difficult for her to feel or express them verbally. During one session, she drew a three picture representation of herself. In one picture, she was a beautiful, graceful ballerina with all the confidence befitting a "star"; in the second picture, she was an extremely angry young woman with a knife in her hand; in the third, she was a tiny, shaking, frightened child being threatened by the woman with the knife.

In her drawings, Joan had unconsciously depicted the many conflicting feelings about the self which individuals affected by parental alcoholism often struggle with. The first picture, the ballerina, represents the part of the person that faces the world as the "ego ideal," the "ideal child" or the "bad child." This part mirrors through images the child develops — the past hopes, dreams, fears, wishes or nightmares of the parent or parents. Her second picture, that of the angry young woman, represents the severe depression beneath the surface image or ego ideal, i.e., the punitive, demanding internalized parent who is constantly pushing for and demanding more perfection or more failure. The picture of the tiny, frightened child represents the disowned child's part of the self — that part of the ego that was never allowed the freedom of emotional development. It includes the tears never cried, the fears

never expressed, all of the child's normal emotional responses. These responses have been imprisoned by a superficial image which allowed for "attention," but not acceptance or love in the fullest sense of the word.

Although the impact of parental alcoholism on child development is mediated by a host of factors, it would be fair to say that most children growing up in alcoholic homes are affected developmentally. In many cases, children raised by parents who are Adult Children of alcoholics, even though they have not followed parental patterns of drinking or drug abuse, pass on the effects of delayed grief to their children. As stated by one Adult Child trying to raise her own children without what she called "the unconscious book on how to be a parent," "Alcoholism is the gift that goes on giving unto the third and fourth generation."

It is impossible to make statements about the effect of parental alcoholism on child development which apply equally to all children growing up in alcoholic homes. Many factors need to be taken into consideration. Some of these factors are: the degree to which the parent or parents focus on the developmental needs of the children rather than on the addiction or the effects of addiction; whether one or both parents are alcoholic; pre-existing pathology, if any, in the parent, parents, and/or family system; which parent is alcoholic and the non-alcoholic parent's response to the illness; the stage of alcoholism the parent is experiencing and how the alcoholism or addiction is manifested; when in the child's developmental history a parent or parents is/are alcoholic; the presence or absence of other supportive family members, parents, substitutes or siblings, and the amount of emotional energy from the parent/parents that is available to the child rather than expended on repression and denial of unfinished griefwork left over from the parents' own childhoods.

In examining Joan's early history, several factors affected her early development. First was the effect of her mother's delayed grief from her own childhood. Because her mother had not come to terms with never having become a ballerina, she made Joan, early in the child's development, an object of her personal narcissistic fulfillment, rather than a freely developing child in her own right.

Second, Joan had little recall of her father, who was absent from home most of the time. He was a salesman who was on the road a great deal and when he was at home, he was unavailable because he was either drinking or involved in his own world in the "den." What she did remember were the chaotic times when in alcoholic rage he would focus his abusiveness on her younger brother. The boy became an object of her father's disappointments in himself and his own life. Although he never hit Joan, she was a witness to her brother being abused, and thus, a secondary victim of the abuse. She felt emotionally responsible for her brother and therefore responsible for the beatings. Although she frequently tried to distract her father through entertainment or "clowning," her attempts were usually futile. Joan felt added guilt because her father constantly said she was "the apple of his eye." Although she had no real relationship of substance with her father, his added focus on her as the "special child" caused her a great deal of alienation in her relationship with her brother. Her mother responded to her special status in a hostile, competitive manner.

Third, the focus of both parents seemed to be on the repression and denial of their own early childhood disappointments or on avoiding acknowledging her father's active alcoholism and her mother's developing alcoholism.

Fourth, the family was extremely isolated — neither parent had a network of friends, and Joan and her brother developed few peer relationships and seldom felt comfortable bringing home the few friends they had.

Fifth, because neither parent was emotionally available, either consciously or unconsciously, Joan and her brother received little "parenting" in the true sense. Instead, they became objects of their parents' needs and projections. There was little or none of the validation of their feelings and emotions necessary for the development of a real self (or ego), only an emphasis by the parents on projected images (ego ideal). There was no safe place for these children to work through or master the traumas faced in everyday life, let alone validation or support for feelings stimulated by the family's focus on addiction, and little or no buffering or protection of these children's young egos. Both Joan and her brother became "adults" early. Her brother became the "cause" of drinking and anger in the family and Joan became the "savior" of wounded images. Their developmental process was put "on hold."

Children such as Joan and her brother forego their own developmental processes and become prisoners to the mirror projections of their injured parents, thus making it impossible to either develop their own true sense of self or to go through the normal emotional separation from their parents either in early childhood or later in normal adolescent development. As stated by Alice Miller (1981, p.13).

"The difficulties inherent in experiencing and developing one's own emotions lead to bond permanence, which prevents individuation, in which both parties have an interest. The parents have found in their child's false self the confirmation they were looking for, a substitute for their own missing structures; the child, who has been unable to build up his own structures, is first consciously and then unconsciously (through the introject) dependent on his parents."

**The Healthy Family**

At this point, we will examine the development of a child raised in a healthy family and compare normal childhood development with that of Joan and her brother. In discussing normal child development, we are relying extensively on the work of Selma Fraiberg (1959), Margaret Mahler (1968), Alice Miller (1981), Heinz Kohut (1971), and D.W. Winnicott (1965).

For the sake of comparison, we will give the children raised in our hypothetical healthy family the names of Sally and Tom. Sally and Tom's parents describe their partnership as a happy one. They have each retained their own sense of identity in the relationship, each with their own professions, friends

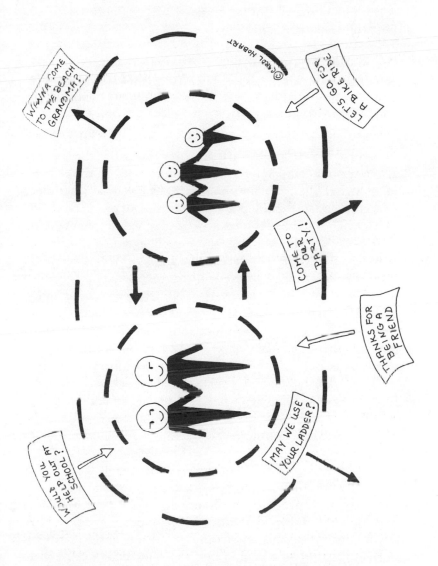

and supportive network. They support each other's development as adults, enjoy their fun times together, experience
conflicts from time to time and say that arguments throughout
their history as a couple have strengthened the bond of
intimacy in their relationship rather than create distance.
They state that their relationship is one of choice rather than
need, and they feel continued renewal in their original commitment as they develop as adults. They discussed having
children before they formed their partnership, and each
agreed that it was an important part of their future life
together. Both felt the support of their families in this decision
and welcomed the arrival of their first child, Sally.

They both acknowledged that along with the joy that Sally
brought to their relationship in her first year of life, there were
also important adjustments and some stresses on their partnership. Each had to make changes in their normal schedules
to accommodate a child. Sally's needs were of prime concern
to both. They worked out routines and schedules that would
satisfy her needs for holding, bathing, changing, feeding, etc.,
as well as times that they each could have to themselves, and
times they could have together with the help of their respective
families. They proudly showed early pictures taken of Sally
and talked about the aspects of her that resembled each of
them and parts of her appearance and personality which were
distinctly her own. They eagerly watched for her first smile
and debated over whether it was in fact recognition of mother
or "gas." They took turns picking her up when she cried,
talking to her, walking with her, rocking her and pushing her
stroller on sunny weekend days. Sally was the center of much
of their existence although they were careful to retain their
commitment to each other and to themselves.

With the onset of walking came new demands from Sally
—a beginning of a type of independence yet unmastered. They
carefully child-proofed the house for her safety and her
developing needs for exploration. They noticed changes in her
developing personality and would laugh at her antics, at times
mirroring games like peek-a-boo that they had once played
with her. They also found new words entering their interac-

tions with her like caring, yet firm "no's."

In her two's Sally presented a new type of behavior and at times would create stress for her parents. Sally would run ahead of them in the park, laughing as they pretended to struggle to catch up; or she would ask for milk, not accept it, and then ask for juice instead. They soon learned to place the milk on the counter and insist that it was the only choice despite her tears and anger while she insisted on a second choice. They talked her through fear of people and monsters and continued talking with each other about her developing personality and their development as parents. When they saw her terror of a friend's dog, they made it safe for her to observe the animal while they protected her from its overwhelming size.

When Sally was three, her brother, Tommy, was born, which made Sally none too happy. They listened to her excitement at having a brother as well as her wish-filled fantasy stories of the monster taking baby brother away, letting her know in her own language that ambivalence regarding a new younger brother was to be expected. They read her books on "a new baby in the family," and took turns meeting both Tommy's developing needs and Sally's needs for continued nurturing, protection and attention.

New stresses were added to their little family as well as continued need for time together as a couple for fun and conflict resolution. They recognized new needs for understanding, yet limits as the children developed and sibling rivalry came into full swing and new experiences unfolded —like Sally's first day at school. They learned the magic balance of holding children close and setting limits through understanding, yet letting go at the same time.

Their own parents had modeled this for them from their early childhood through adolescence as well as the important skill of conflict resolution during the developmental process. Sally and Tom's mother related a story of the first time she learned that magic balance; Tom was four years old when she made his finding his own shoes a prerequisite for his visiting a neighborhood friend. He refused to look for his shoes, had a tantrum, and insisted that she find them for him. The struggle continued until it was too late to visit his friend. She held him and listened to his sadness at the missed occasion, yet kept the limit even though she would have enjoyed some quiet time that afternoon for herself. She acknowledged to her partner later, "It's not easy raising kids. Sometimes it feels like a full-time job."

Raising children most definitely is, at times, "a full-time job" as is, at times, earning a living, continuing to develop a relationship with one's partner and friends, as well as attending to one's own adult development process. Continuing one's own adult development in the face of life stresses, while continuing the expansion of supportive networks for one's self, while parenting full-time sometimes feels like an impossible task as anyone can attest who has raised children from birth to the age of eighteen. If, however, one adds to this already difficult task, alcoholism and/or delayed grief from one's childhood losses, attending to the healthy normal development of children is almost an impossibility.

## The Difference: Focus on Children vs. Focus on Alcohol

What do we see when comparing the developmental process in Sally and Tom's family with that of Joan and her brother? It is apparent that Sally and Tom were the central focus of their parents' lives. Their needs were attended to, their words and pre-verbal behaviors were a focus of parental attention and concern. Joan and her brother, on the other hand, became objects of their parents' unmet or repressed emotions or desires. They became the band-aids for their parents' wounded ego development, as quite possibly their parents had been for their grandparents. As Joan related the early history of her brother and herself, it was obvious that there were two foci in her family: One, the necessity for her parents to parent themselves through their children, rather than the reverse; and two, the focus on drinking and addictive behaviors. Joan related as early as age five being left to take care

of her brother in a motel room while her parents, in another, celebrated an occasion she couldn't remember. Early in treatment, Joan recounted deep feelings of guilt for an injury to her brother which occurred while trying to put him into his nightclothes, her feelings of inadequacy in trying to find their parents, and subsequently both getting punished for not being "good kids." She felt failure for not being a good mother before she was six years of age, and it was not until later in treatment that she could connect the above incident with feelings of overwhelming fear and abandonment. Only when it was safe could she afford to allow the terrified child within any expression of feeling rather than preserving the stoic, fearless adult she had mirrored for her mother. Joan had decided prior to treatment, as do many Adult Children, that she could never trust herself to have her own children because she would be a "bad mother."

Sally and Tom's parents began their relationship as fully developed individuals with choices and ego strengths which were the by-products of their own emotional nourishment as children. They made decisions as individuals and discussed them. They made decisions as a couple regarding the family and effective parenting. They established a parental unit and supported each other, thus allowing their children to be "children" and to form their own unit of sibling support which could be free of adult worries. Hence, both Tom and Sally could later individuate from their parents without worry and guilt about separation.

Joan's parents came to the marriage with ego deficits as adults. The fabric of their family was determined by reactions to crisis, projections of parental disappointment and parental inadequacies onto the children, addictive cycles or early failed attempts at trauma mastery by individual adults in pain, rather than by parents who could form a healthy coalition for intimacy and parenting. At age five Joan became not only her mother's object of unmet needs but a parent to her brother. Her brother became not only the projection of his father's disowned negative self-image but also the child of a five-year-old caring, but ill-equipped sister. Because the children became extensions of their parents' injured egos, they remained bonded to their parents and could not form their own sibling sub-system. Their fear of abandonment and the loss of the only "self" that had been allowed expression or development — the self projected by the parent — prohibited each of them from individuating and eventually emotionally separating from them.

In Sally and Tom's family, limits were consistent and were maintained. The children could learn what was expected on a consistent basis, which then allowed them to not only develop their own internal limits (super-ego) but also to internalize their parents as appropriate role models.

In Joan and her brother's upbringing, nothing was consistent. Limits were randomly set and withdrawn based on parental need or whim from moment to moment or determined by levels of sobriety or intoxication. What became internalized in both of these children was a rigid, angry parent who randomly rejected behavior and rather than setting limits for impulses, drives, or emotions, rejected the whole of the developing child, thereby resulting in the development of an overly-rigid and anxiety-laden conscience (super-ego) that restricted choice and spontaneity.

As stated so well by Alice Miller, "An adult can only be fully aware of his/her feelings if he/she has internalized an affectionate and empathetic self-object (parent)." (Miller 1981, p. 20) Sally and Tom's parents not only passed on to their children an empathetic response but also were able to recognize their own needs as adults and fulfill them rather than expecting unconditional love from their mates or children. They each had an active, supportive network of friends outside of the partnership as well as support from their own parents to traverse stressful life situations. They did not expect all of their needs to be met within the family.

This active, supportive network was not available or established in Joan's family. Her parents had very few friendships and those they did have were oftentimes "drinking buddies." Both parents had extremely poor relationships with their own parents and felt interactions with them increased stress in their lives rather than lessened it. Joan remembered constant fights between her parents. Each blamed the other or the children for problems in their lives; each expected unexpressed needs to be met magically as if other family members could "mind-read," and if those needs weren't met, punishment followed. Joan was expected to be her mother's counselor or confidante from a very early age, listening to stories of how her father had ruined her mother's life and her mother's protests that she had stayed with him "for the sake of the children." She also heard her father's recurrent accusations of how her mother had "driven him to drink." The spoken or unspoken message that Joan heard loud and clear was that it was her responsibility not only to make each parent happy but also to mend the marriage that was being "saved" for her. No one in her family took responsibilty for goals or happiness. No one talked directly to the other, and conflict, rather than being "healthy," was instead something which would result in abandonment and more frustration.

Sally's parents served as her protective buffer from the world. They protected her from frightening experiences, such as the neighborhood dog, whenever possible, and comforted her when she was hurt. Joan was the protective buffer for her parents, breaking up their fights, and being their "respectable image" for the outside world. They did not protect her from the traumas of childhood and, instead, often created the terrors that invaded her nighttime dreams.

**The Bill of Rights**

A child at birth has a "human bill of rights" — the right to be an object of unconditional parental love; the right, for a time, to be the center of parental attention and to have needs met without request. A child has the right for consistency, limits, security, warmth and understanding. A child has the right to be loved for what he or she is rather than for being what others wish him/her to be or become. A child has the right to be parented and nurtured rather than falling under the emormous weight of making up for the losses of her/his parents. A child has the right to be protected from traumatic situations and stresses which are burdensome to a developing ego.

Children raised in alcoholic or drug-addicted families forego these basic rights as children in exchange for merely the right to "survive," and frequently spend the rest of their lives attempting to recapture from others in their adult lives (their partners, their children, their professions) the love that they so desperately needed in the past. They consistently attempt, through recreations of their past, mastery of the trauma of having never been a child so that they can "catch up" with their peers in the attainment of merely the "right to be." Sally will move on to mastery of stages in adult development while Joan still attempts to recover from the losses of childhood.

Many Adult Children are fiercely "counterdependent," attempting at all times to "stay in control," and don't accept basic needs in themselves for comforting or support, while at the same time ignoring the power of their own accomplishments. They may become extremely anxious when it is suggested by friends, partners, or therapists, that they make decisions based on their own needs, not someone else's, or that possibly they could say "no" to the demands of others.'

Szretsky (1985) in his description of the "anxiety of being in control," believes that the fear of feeling oneself as truly independent of the needs, wishes, and desires of others is the terror of finally feeling the abandonment of the parent. If, in fact, the Adult Child perceives himself as an individual making choices and accomplishing tasks based on his needs rather than through the desires of others, he would feel the loss of the parent that needed him. Szretsky characterizes this fear by using the metaphor of the old Bugs Bunny cartoon: "In the old Bugs Bunny cartoon, Bugs Bunny defies the law of gravity by running over the face of the cliff and just keeps running. He only falls when he realizes what he's done and remembers what he was supposed to be capable of." (Szretsky 1985, p. 53). Many Adult Children seek in their partner what was never received from their parents and experience relationships as "addictions" rather than "choices."

These Adult Children seek to establish lost self-esteem

through seeking the total and unconditional love of a partner, or through "constant external affirmation." (Berkowitz 1985) They attempt to regain from a partner what they never received in normal childhood development from parents. Without the affirmation of self from their partner, they feel depressed, suicidal and that they have lost themselves. This leads to a sense of desperateness in relationships and a frequent inability to detach from a love relationship in which they have been repeatedly rejected. They are often surprised that when they finally attain commitment from a person who was sought almost as an addiction that loneliness re-emerges; they feel oddly detached and "out of love" again, and go seeking another unattainable relationship. As explained by Berkowitz: "The aggrandized object is often needed with an addiction-like intensity. Without the attachment to an admired object, these individuals may report feeling incomplete, not whole, lost or empty. Since the object is external to the self, even its possession can no more than temporarily repair the internal sense of emptiness with which the patient is struggling." (Berkowitz, 1985 p. 233)

When listening to the conflicts of Adult Children in marital or relationship counseling, the therapist often can hear the need for the completion of those developmental stages lost in childhood when it is suggested that a partner know what is needed without those needs being stated: "You would have done that if you loved me without my always telling you what I need," or "I never feel accepted by you no matter how hard I try or what I do — there is always something you criticize." The unconditional love and acceptance which is a "right" in childhood is frustratingly not attainable in a friendship or marriage. Without grieving that tremendous loss from the past, it is impossible to regain mastery of the present, and Adult Children find themselves locked in repetitive relationship patterns, much like an actor type-cast into a part in a play that never ends.

In some cases, Adult Children who were consistently verbally and physically abused in childhood repetitively seek an even more destructive merger with partners in an attempt to attain a precarious self-identity based on their relationship with a parent in childhood. Rather than seeking constant approval or attempting to act out the needs of partners to avoid feeling the abandonment of the parent in the past, they seek punishment. It is often confusing when a counselor is confronted with a client who is exceptionally talented, extremely sensitive to the needs of others, and appears to have a great deal of ego-strength, yet also engages in self punishment through self mutilation, repetitive suicide attempts, and repetitive patterns of highly self-destructive abusive relationships. It is possible to view such consistent self-destructive acts as an attempt to survive and protect a fragile balance of self. Montgomery (1985) agrees with this particular view of survival adaption and sees the self-destructive acts of the individual as attempts to maintain a unity with the parent in much the same way as an individual constantly trying to meet the needs of others.

She sees the self-punitive acts as a way to feel connected and maintain the self image developed in childhood rather than to feel the pain of dissolution and abandonment.

"The pain, the cutting, the burning, even the suicide are attempts at repairing the cohesiveness of the self in the face of overwhelming anxiety associated with dissolution." (Montgomery, 1985, p. 506)

The relationship formed with the parent in this case is one of the punisher and the punished. The child, as in the other examples, is again the object of the parent's needs, only in this case it isn't the parent's need for an "ideal child" but rather a child through whom the parents could mirror the punishment of the self. If the only relationship formed with a parent is one of acceptance through being the object of punishment, then this self punishment becomes also a survival adaption. As stated by one individual, "I guess if you are a victim, you're never alone." (Montgomery, 1985, p.509).

Unfortunately, alcoholism is the gift that goes on giving into the third and fourth generation. The band-aids for parental wounds are frequently their own children. This developmental legacy is prominent in all families who share unresolved trauma and grief and manifests itself as the proverbial "elephant in the living room." Sometimes the "elephant" is the result of being born in this country to immigrants who have had difficulty adapting or grieving the loss of homeland; sometimes, the children of individuals who survived the holocaust of World War II; and sometimes, parents who smother their own children with "over parenting" because of their lack of sense of self or debilitating depression. The authors agree with James Herzog when he says: "Experience with other survivor-parents lends strong presumptive evidence to the notion that unbound, unintegrated, and unshared trauma is most likely to overflow. The very acts of caretaking, as well as the affective climate, then become the medium for the message. Without intervention, a relatively stable chain of transmissions can occur. We are seeing not only survivors' children, but also their grandchildren, in whom there are manifestations of such a legacy." (1982, p. 110)

It takes an inordinate amount of psychic energy to separate out memories that are tolerable from those that are intolerable. The psychic energy invested in excessive denial and repression is energy that is not available to a survivor parent for the raising of his/her own children. The energy expended by a child in the repression and denial of traumatic memory or in the construction of fantasy parents to provide the nurturing that unavailable, detached, or enmeshed parents cannot give is physically expensive. This energy is stolen from the process of the child's primary task of being a child, i.e., developing a sense of self, exploring, and individuating. The child who lacks nurturing and is unable to separate from and internalize the parental object is only capable of enmeshment, bond permanence, or detachment in new family relationships.

"The literature directed to the survivor parent-child relationship has produced a broad range of characterizations that include emotional unavailability, overprotectiveness, vicarious living through the lives of children, inhibitions of separation, inhibitions of guilt, . . ." (Prince, 1975, p.12)

And the unconscious gifts of generations go on giving.

Chapter Three

# When You Lean on People Who Lean on Bottles, They Fall Over

Loss and the attendant feelings of sorrow and sadness which loss evokes are integral parts of the human condition. Sorrow and feelings of sadness are normal emotional responses to loss and abate with time as the individual "works through" the loss and adjusts to his or her changed life circumstances. The emotional process of "working through" a loss is called "griefwork." The individual is said to be grieving, mourning, or in a state of bereavement, and the multitude of feelings which loss evokes is called "grief." Grief is experienced as mental anguish or emotional pain and is the psyche's response to a wound to the individual's sense of well-being.

Loss and its consequent threat to self-esteem and feelings of integrity and well-being evokes a wide array of emotional reactions: shock, numbness, denial, anguish, crying, protest, depression, sadness, despair, guilt, anger, yearning, pining, aimless wandering, bargaining and feelings of helplessness and hopelessness. Usually, there is a precipitating event which signals a real or threatened loss; the individual's response is proportionate to the magnitude of the loss and his emotional responses to the loss are time limited and follow a pattern which will eventuate in the resolution of his sadness. His feelings of sorrow gradually lessen as he acknowledges the reality of the loss, feels the emotions/pain associated with it, accepts that no amount of denial or bargaining or manipulation will restore that which has been lost, and eventually becomes willing to move on to other attachments. However, in the "depression-prone" individual, such is not the case.

A current loss can trigger the onset of a downward emotional spiral in which the individual is overtaken by a pervasive, depressed mood, a sense of despair and pessimism, and vehement self-rebuke. It is as if there were a file in the individual's unconscious mind marked "loss," and each successive loss has the power to access the file and open old wounds, especially those having to do with irretrievable losses of significant relationships in the past.

Chapters One and Two of this book focus on the survival adaption that children in alcoholic families develop as a defense against the pervasive sense of loss engendered by a capricious, unpredictable and sometimes violent environment. In this chapter, the authors will more closely examine the concept of "depression-proneness" and discuss problems of depression as related to incomplete sorrow work. Let's first begin by asking several questions about depression. "There are many data that suggest that genetic and biochemical factors play a role in this disorder, but whether they are etiologic, contributory, or predisposing is yet to be clarified." (Salzman, 1975, p. 43) Is depression a universal reaction to loss to which all individuals are susceptible at one time or another, or are certain individuals more at risk, more vulnerable to the onset of depression consequent to a loss? To answer this question, we must look first at how the term "depression" is commonly used.

"Depression" is often employed to describe a wide array of disordered mood states which range from the Monday morning "blahs" and feelings of disappointment when things just don't work out to those severely depressed states which are totally immobilizing and life-threatening. Depression on feelings of sadness and disappointment are normal responses to loss, usually tend to be transient, and to resolve fairly quickly. Hence, some feelings of depression are a normal consequence of grief reactions and losses and are part of the developmental adventure of life. When, however, one's response to loss is more intense and of longer duration than the precipitating event would seem to merit, and when one's self-esteem is severely diminished as a response to loss with attendant feelings of pessimism, futility, self-reproach, guilt, and anger turned against the self, then we are describing one of the manifestations of "depressive disorder." Thus, although all humans react to loss with sadness and a depressed mood, not all individuals react with a tendency toward a depressive disorder. Joan's depression would not have been as severe had she been grieving only the trauma of a current injury and the temporary loss of employment. It was the fact that Joan's current loss of the ability to dance stimulated the opening of an entire file of previously ungrieved childhood losses that led her to the depth of suicidal depression. Our concern in this chapter is with this predisposition for depression which has been fostered by certain early life environments, e.g., those environments which are "depressogenic" rather than "ego-bolstering." (Flach, 1975, p.8).

Alcoholic families have been characterized as being similar to living with an air raid a day, an exampe of persistent, unabating, cumulative life stress. There is a rich research literature which links depression and life stress, particularly stress generated by loss, either real or threatened. Depressed subjects in one study reported three times more stressful life events in the six months preceding the onset of depression than did controls. (Paykel, 1975, p. 59) Although there is little empirical research on the effects of stressful situations which are persistent rather than new events and changes (Paykel, 1975, p. 63), clinical impressions would indicate that environments characterized by persistent stress are "depressogenic" and contribute to the development in some individuals of a personality which is vulnerable and "loss sensitive."

"Life events bear a causal relationship to the onset of most depressions and probably to a greater extent than with most other psychiatric disorders. A variety of types of events are implicated. Most prominent among these are separations and interpersonal losses. It is clear, however, that depression is a response to a wide range of events with threatening implications, including blows to the self-esteem, interpersonal discord, events that are socially undesirable, and major disruptions in life pattern." (Paykel, 1975, p. 70)

It appears that "depression-proneness" is a possible outcome when an established early life attachment/relationship is disrupted, whereas the outcome is quite different if there is a failure to form attachment bonds, *i.e.*, sociopathy. The need to attach to a primary figure is evidently a basic drive, not only in humans, but also in other species. A state of "object constancy" has been achieved when the developing human organism is able to hold in his mind a mental representation of the absent person and trusts that that person will return, even though he/she is not actually physically present at that moment. In so doing, the child "internalizes" the object/attachment figure along with that person's characteristics, qualities and attitudes, especially those held toward the infant. The outcome of this process can be either adverse, beneficial, or both, depending on what is internalized.

One's "self-feeling" or self-regard initially is derived from reflections of attitudes held towards the self by the parent/parents. The "looking glass self" contains positive appraisals which the child internalizes as feelings of "I'm lovable, worthwhile, and valuable" if, in fact, the parent is excited about and prepared to welcome the child into her life. However, the outcome of this process of internalization can be adverse, especially when difficult life circumstances intervene, making it impossible for the parent either to fully welcome the child or provide it with quality care and affection. Such is often the case in alcoholic families where either the mother, the primary attachment figure, is pre-empted by her alcoholism or is pre-empted by her response to spousal alcoholism, which may include depression and feelings of immobilization.

Psychodynamic authors often attribute the development of depressive disorders to a discrepancy between the individual's ego ideal or ideal self and real self. The ideal self is the internalization of parental attitudes, beliefs, values and reflected appraisals of the child, i.e., the end product of his relationship with primary objects or attachment figures from his early childhood.

John Bowlby accounts for an individual's tendency to respond in specific ways to loss in terms of a discrepancy between what he calls one's ". . . representational models of attachment figures and of the self that he has built during his childhood and adolescence, and . . . these in turn are a function of the experiences he had in his family during those years. What his actual responses prove then to be turns on the interaction of conditions that surround and follow a loss with the cognitive biases to respond in certain ways that he brings to it . . . in particular, I agree that the part played by the kinds of childhood experience a person has had are critical. For, through the medium of his representational models, they are in large part responsible, first for the patterns of affectional relationship he makes during his life and, secondly, for the cognitive biases he brings to any loss he may sustain." (Bowlby, 1980, p. 232-233)

Alcoholic families are characterized by denial and operate on the belief, e.g., "There is nothing wrong here. Don't talk about it." (Stephanie Brown, 1983, Los Angeles) For a child still forming representational models of his parents, this constitutes a dilemma. The message from his parents may be that they are above reproach and are to be idealized. Their behavior is descrepant with the child's experience of them and the child resolves the discrepancy by faulting his own perceptions and feelings, a Charlie Brown syndrome of "I have no one to blame but myself."

Since alcoholism often generates capricious, unpredictable behavior in both the alcoholic and the co-dependent spouse who is developing her/his own "mirror" illness, children in these families often experience repeated disappointments in displays of parental affection, thereby exaggerating their emotional need for attachment and affection and rendering them vulnerable to feelings of disappointment. Such children develop a derivative sense of self, *e.g.*, "You're nobody 'til somebody loves you," in that their self-esteem comes to be dependent on external narcissistic supplies or sources of gratification. Self-esteem in these youngsters is tenuous since it is dependent on the rising and falling tide of attention and approval of significant attachment figures. As a consequence, they are deficient in self-soothing and self-caring behaviors, *i.e.*, healthy sources of self-gratification, and tend to reach for behaviors which are ego syntonic in meeting their needs, *i.e.*, those behaviors which both gratify and punish simultaneously such as daydreaming, eating, overconscientiousness, and in later life possibly drugs, alcohol, gambling, and workaholism.

*I try to suppress*
*that as an adult,*
*I abandoned the child within.*
*The little girl locked inside,*
*beating frantically against my breast.*
*Begging to be heard.*
*The child*
*whose tears were never seen*
*whose screams were never heard*
*whose fear was ignored*
*whose anger was never validated.*

*What of the 15 year old*
*who stands*
*behind the child?*
*Waiting patiently*
*for her rage to be expressed.*

*The sullen, brooding product*
  *of an alcoholic father*
  *a behavior-disordered mother*
  *two rapists*
  *and*
  *her*
  *own*
  *self-abuse.*

*Sitting quietly*
*observing the little girl*
*as well as the adolescent,*
*knowing her turn*
*may never materialize*
*is an anorexic 23 year old*
*woman/child.*

*She bears scars and blemishes*
  *of 5 years of physical, sexual*
  *and emotional abuse.*

*She aches*
*to bellow*
*that*
*she*
*hurts. . . .*
*But she remains silent.*
*She knows.*
*She must be a good little girl.*

*Now standing before the mirror*
*is a not unpretty woman.*
*She labels herself.*
*She is extremely critical,*

*A perfectionist to a fault*
*knowing each and everyone*
*of her defects.*

*Her intellect*
*understands these*
*others exist within her.*
*But to acknowledge their pain is*
*terrifying.*

*Her feelings are confused,*
*because of their quantity*
*and scope.*
*They sometimes escape*
*and she feels*
*crazy.*

*She writes frantically*
*seeking release.*
*Trying to make them*
*disappear.*
*Identification*
*too difficult*
*at times.*

*She tries to fit*
*that time worn mask*
*on her face.*
*The one that says,*
*"I am*
*Fine*
*Strong*
*Normal*
*with no feelings."*

*But the facade*
*is no longer workable*
*uncomfortable, even.*
*It just doesn't fit*
*She is sad.*
*A tear slides down her cheek.*

— *Nanci Presley-Holley*
*8/29/85*

Many Adult Children's early memories are of themselves alone in the house eating a bag of cookies or being "befriended" by a chocolate cake. Oftentimes early childhood diaries contain statements like: "My mom loved me today because I helped her with the dusting" or "Dad was mad at me today because I lost the baseball game. I didn't mean to hurt my dad, I won't do so bad tomorrow." When significant attachment figures fail to provide the attention, appreciation, or affection that these youngsters need, they rebuke themselves in an attempt to retrieve that which has been lost and as expiation for the crime which they feel they must have committed for it's having been withheld. These children silently feel somehow deficient for being deemed so worthless, unlovable and discardable, and it never consciously occurs to them that in their blind, unswerving loyalty and attachment to their parents that the deficiency lies in the parents, not in the child.

The behavior of children raised in alcoholic families is reminiscent of the experiments conducted by Harry Harlow on attachment and parenting behavior in rhesus monkeys in which the mother monkeys, having themselves not been appropriately parented, not only failed to parent their offspring, but were also rejecting and severely abusive to them. The baby monkey's response to being repeatedly pushed away and beaten was to frantically dash to the mother and desparately cling to her fur. If John Bolby is correct, the human child in such a circumstance does not allow himself to "know" that his environment is deficient in meeting his needs but instead develops two parallel representational models of the parents' behavior, one which the parents demand to be developed in order for the child not to be subject to serious sanctions for failing to see the parents as they need to be seen, and a second representational model which reflects in fact how the child is experiencing the parents and the environment. Since these models are discrepant, the child will be subject to considerable unconscious conflict in attempting to reconcile two such opposing views.

When Adult Children of alcoholics begin coming to terms with having been affected by parental alcoholism, they often experience feeling "crazy" and confused since they cannot trust that they "know" what in fact was true about their childhood, as these two discrepant models shift in and out of conscious awareness. They are frequently overwhelmed with feelings of guilt and shame for entertaining such notions about their parents, and the Mafia-like code of loyalty and family credo of "Don't talk, Don't trust, Don't feel" and "Family Business is Family Business" can acutely exacerbate these feelings of shame and feared reprisal, *e.g.*, being orphaned or cast out emotionally from one's family. (Black, 1982)

According to Bowlby, a number of circumstances can contribute to "depression-proneness." One set can eventuate in chronic mourning, *i.e.*, the failure to complete and resolve one's sorrow work, and the other set of circumstances eventuating in the apparent absence of grieving. Several life positions on the part of a parent can contribute to chronic mourning in a child. Included would be the parent whose underlying message as succinctly stated by Jael Greenleaf is "I'm glad you're here. Take care of me." (Greenleaf, 1984) One can speculate that this parent is herself/himself developmentally incomplete and has not been able to work through the grief attendant to the failure of her/his parents having been incapable of appropriate, supportive parenting. Children born to such a parent feel they are obligated to not only totally take care of the parent but also to be the primary source of validation and self-esteem for her/him. Such parents do not "have children," but instead, operating out of their own sense of emptiness, incompleteness, yearning, bitterness, and an attitude of entitlement and expectation of reparations for wrongs done to them, "take hostages."

Another parental life position which predisposes the child to chronic mourning is one in which the parent's underlying message is "Your behavior can make me sick, crazy, or kill me." Children in these families tend to idealize their saintly, long-suffering parents, and live with acute anxiety that they will "step on a crack and break their mother's back." They are truly the children who come to believe that their normal feelings of aggression and lack of "goodness" are lethal, and they often become very repressed, restricted, anxious, compliant, hypervigilant, "anger phobic" children. The underlying threat of both of these parental life positions is one of abandonment and/or annihilation, i.e., "I will die if you don't take care of me, leaving you with no one," or "You can kill me with your lack of goodness and then you'll be all alone." For a child for whom attachment literally equals survival, it's too big a risk to chance.

The last parental life position is one wherein the parent constantly threatens to desert or commit suicide, leaving the child not only feeling that affection and caring are conditional, but that at any time the parent can punitively retaliate for the child's failure to please by the ultimate "pulling the rug" out from under him. All of the above leave the child feeling ". . . first, a longing for love that has never been met and, next, bitter resentment against those who, for whatever reason, have not given it to him." (Bowlby, 1980, p. 239)

Paradoxically, one of the manifestations of "depression-proneness" in adulthood is the absence of grief and the concomitant presence of behaviors which are considered to be "depressive equivalents," e.g., chronic pain, somatic complaints, alcoholism, drug abuse, and obesity. The developmental histories of such individuals are often characterized by attachment figures who met the child's need for nurturing and comfort with sarcasm, ridicule, and shaming. Such children learn not to expect comfort from others but instead to expect blame, punishment or indifference in the face of distress. They cannot allow themselves to feel their chronic, underlying feeling of depression and instead in adulthood develop behaviors which are misfired attempts at self-soothing and self-care, *e.g.*, drinking, drugging, eating. Early on, these children learn that when they *leaned on people who leaned on bottles, they fell over*, and hence, it was safer to learn to forego the need for comfort and closeness and to become compulsively self-reliant. Oftentimes these individuals have so effectively deactivated their attachment behaviors and become so cut off in their underlying feelings of yearning, that they appear to be immune to feeling anything in the face of loss. Rather than feeling sad, they experience existential despair or are aloof, cool, and appear to feel nothing. Many are people who decided at a very early age to never be vulnerable again, to never cry again and to never need anyone again. They embark on a career of becoming "self-sufficient in an insufficient way" at the terrible personal cost of no longer attaching to others or letting them get close. (Bowlby, 1980, p. 237-242)

Malquist's *deprivation hypothesis* posits "depression-proneness" as a consequence of ". . . disruptions in the (individual's) capacity to form consistent human attachments based on affection." (Malquist, 1975, p. 74) When attachment bonds are disrupted, all individuals respond to this disruption in a four-stage process of numbness, protest, despair and detachment. (Malquist discussing Bowlby, 1975, p. 84) Behaviors which humans share with other species in this *response to loss* sequence include crying, motoric restlessness, angry protests designed to bring back that which has been lost, feelings of yearning, withdrawal, apathy, and despair. The concept of *never* is difficult for any of us to countenance and for a child to feel that he will *never* receive the warmth, attention, and affection he yearns for from significant attachment figures is impossible to accept. Initially the child engages in problem-solving behaviors with his environment, trying to wrest from it what he needs and has lost from it. The persistence of these efforts, according to Malquist, has four potential pathological outcomes:

1. Persistent, unconscious yearnings to recover the lost object which appear surprising clinically since there is an absence of apparent grief.
2. Angry reproaches against the self and other objects in an attempt to regain that which has been lost. This can be accompained by displacement of reproachful behavior unto objects which are inappropriate, i.e., "mourning at a distance." Such displacement may be due to the chronic provocation of anger with no avenue for its release.
3. Development of compulsive care-taking of others and hypersensitivity to the sufferings of others, i.e., the "bird with a broken wing" syndrome, while oblivious to one's own pain (vicarious mourning).
4. Denial of the permanency/irretrievability on a conscious level of that which has been lost, i.e., "Say it isn't so." (Malquist, 1975, p. 84-85)

All of the above bode ill for the child, especially if the feelings surrounding object loss becomes disconnected from the source of the anguish. The child can become "stuck" emotionally and experience chronic feelings of emptiness, emotional hunger, yearning, restlessness as if searching for he knows not what, apathy, anger, detachment, and despair, but without a context to make sense of these feelings. "It's just how I am" is what he deduces, and feeling at an unconscious level discarded, worthless and unlovable. "I brought it on myself; it's all I deserve."

Even when a parent with the best of all intentions wishes to "do right" by his/her children, circumstances can intervene to interfere with attachment bonds and the emotional resolution of their disruption. Children born to depressed parents are exposed to an emotionally contagious, "depressogenic" environment. The child responds, as we all do in the face of someone else's depressed mood, by feeling somehow responsible for it, a failure, a disappointment. The child becomes habituated to the depressed mood which characterizes his home and does not expect others to be interested in him or respond to him. In a sense, he is on the beginning leg of a *chronic stress career* which, since it overwhelms his developing ego's capacity to integrate and adapt to such a high magnitude of loss, will render him later in life hypersensitive to the slightest rebuff and easily overwhelmed by the slightest frustration. His computer will say "error" at what seems on the outside like the slightest provocation, but what we can't see is that on the inside, the provocation was just one more of thousands of cumulative experiences of loss.

### Shannon

*Blonde hair, brown eyes*
*Gentle as a butterfly*
*Tiny feet*
*Even smaller hands*
*She is mine.*

*Days pass.*
*My baby grows*
*Bald as an eagle*
*Lashes divine*
*Giggles and bubbles*
*The world is fine.*

*Months fly by.*
*My daughter walks*
*"Ma-ma, ma-ma"*
*Take my hand,*
*Let me guide your steps.*
*We are one.*

*Years meander*
*Reading and Christmas plays*
*New dresses and red patent leather shoes*
*That awful 6th grade concert*

*Tears and scrapes*
*Laughter and sand castles*
*Kites and boyfriends*
*Horses and camp*
*"Ma-ma, I love you."*

*But something intervened.*
*At thirteen?*
*Or was it at 12?*
*Or was it at 9?*

*This dark, sinister being.*
*This thing, no stranger.*
*It made her forget.*
*All the times I slept*
*When I should have listened.*
*All the times she reached out*
*And I was gone.*
*It eased the pain of the molestation.*
*It erased the terror of the rape.*
*It denied her abandonment*
*And made all things seem but dreams.*

*If I had one wish*
*Or I were a witch*
*I'd turn back the hands of time*
*To that place in space*
*When you were mine.*

*But release you I must.*
*For you are in the grip*
*of one I know only too well.*
*You are one of the million*
*Addicted to a living hell.*

*It comes in coke; in pills,*
*in booze, in pot.*
*And although it eases life's*
*unfairness for a moment*
*In time it destroys*
*dreams, love and lives.*

*And one brown-eyed, blonde daughter of mine.*

**Nanci Presley-Holley**

*5/28/85*

Alcoholism or any other life circumstance which chronically pre-empts parental attention and leads to a state of chronic crisis becoming normalized in the family will have a similar effect on the developing child. Alcoholic and co-alcoholic parents just can't *be there* consistently for their children as reliable attachment figures. In these families, parents often lurch back and forth from being emotionally absent and/or abusive to their children to being overly solicitous and overly involved with them. Children in these families feel literally *jacked around* and live in a world of emotional "feast or famine."

In Chapters One and Two, the authors spoke of the defensive survival adaptation children in dysfunctional families develop. These adaptations are coping responses to experiences of chronic, persistent loss and many variables affect which defenses a child develops. One variable is the child's inborn characteristics or temperament. This is another way of saying not all children of alcoholic parents respond in the same way to their distorted life circumstances. Temperament, birth order, identification with a parent, being part of a parental alliance, when in a child's developmental history alcoholism occurs, which parent is alcoholic; or whether both are alcoholic, how the alcoholism is manifested, what stage the alcoholism has progressed to, the degree of familial isolation from families of origin and the larger community, etc. These are just some of the variables which affect the survival adaptation which the child adopts.

Experiences tend to be more traumatizing in the absence of a comforting and supportive environment. Alcoholic families characteristically are isolated families who are protecting their secret of "There's nothing wrong here. Don't talk about it" from both the inside world of the family, the proverbial "elephant in the living room," and from the outside world. Unless there are "cookie people" in the lives of the children in these families, they experience their terror alone.

Ideally, "cookie people" are substitute attachment figures with whom the child can develop a relationship. Hopefully, they are warm, nurturant people who are tolerant of a wide range of affect expression and are available to listen to and support the traumatized child in talking about what's going on at home. Many Adult Children of alcoholics can look back in time and identify the significant attachment figures or "cookie people" who served as their surrogate parents, role models, friends, protectors and encouragers on their journey from childhood to adulthood. Often their individual sense of self and good self-feeling are a patchwork quilt made up of experiences internalized from these significant interactions.

Individuals for whom there were insufficient mitigating factors in the environment in early childhood come to feel helpless and hopeless about developing affectional relationships, a conclusion they reach as the end result of their experiences with their primary attachment figures. (Bowlby, 1980, p. 247) Such individuals tend to be *depression-prone*, i.e., experience a disordered version of what is a normal emotional process in coming to terms with loss and attendant feelings of sadness. Bowlby attributes three sets of conditions in the family of origin as contributing to *depression-proneness*:

1. The child has done the best he is able in trying to win parental approval and affection, and nothing he does is good enough, leading to any subsequent loss being processed as just another *failure*.

2. The child has been told repeatedly how unlovable, defec-

tive and inadequate he is. He sees all attachment figures as unavailable, punitive, rejecting, and fault-finding and in the face of adversity expects others to attack rather than be helpful.

3. The child is more likely to have actually experienced the loss of a parent in childhood through circumstances over which he has no control, leaving him feeling impotent and powerless to affect any outcome through his own effort. (Bowlby, 1980, p. 247)

The lack of a supportive environment and disruptions in object constancy can lead to the development of a youngster who is pseudomature, precocious, hyper-responsible, overly self-reliant and totally out of touch with his own feelings and conflicts.

Behind the mask of maturity and sophistication hides a frightened child caught between feelings of retaliatory rage, submissive fear, and deep yearning for affection from significant adults in his life. One resolution which he may attempt is to accept that his own goals and expectations will never be acceptable and/or attainable and therefore he forfeits the development of a true sense of self and instead becomes the derivative self that satisfies parental expectations. In the process, the child may become completely disconnected from any awareness of the parental injunction which forbids him from seeing the representational model of his parents as any different from how they wish to be seen and from the prohibition of telling anyone what they in fact were like.

Arieti and Bemporad contend that the child who is destined to become *depression-prone* adopts one of three life positions in attempting to resolve the dilemma. One life position has already been alluded to, namely the youngster develops a pattern of placation and sets about a life course of being compliant and conforming to the perceived expectations of a *Dominant Other*. This usually follows a real or threatened disruption in the child's attachment bonds with that person, with his becoming willing to submit, work hard, and obey in exchange for conditional safety and security. Such a decision proves to be extraordinarily costly for the personality development. All of the individual's actions become predicated on the desire to win the love, applause, and approval of an authority figure, with the child becoming incapable of taking action based on his own wants and needs. He becomes like a tree which is bent more and more in one direction, achieving sometimes the status of *special* or *favorite* child in his family, but with a nagging underlying feeling that his value is as an object to repair his family's damaged self-esteem rather than as himself. (Arieti/Bemporad, 1978, p. 24-25)

*Depression-prone* individuals have overly developed superegos and consciences which usually tend to be harsher and more restrictive than the expectations of the attachment figures who have been internalized. As a result, if their over-conscientiousness and overachievement are not rewarded, they are highly vulnerable to a downward depressive spiral initiated from within by their own self-rebuke and tendency to beat up on themselves emotionally. Their fear of punishment for failure is so extreme that they are afraid that they will literally be attacked if they make a mistake. (Malquist, 1975, p. 86)

The inner emotional life of such a person is characterized by conflict. On the one hand, the individual shows himself to be competitive, perfectionistic and ambitious as the potential avenue to parental approval; on the other hand, he envies others who are not burdened by such onerous superego demands and wishes to avoid provoking their jealousy and both his and their hostility at all costs. He becomes like a dog who, upon encountering a pack of strange dogs, throws himself on the ground and exposes his underbelly as a way of saying, "Don't take me too seriously. I'm just a buffoon. I'm no threat." He needs to compete; yet he shuns competition out of fear of abandonment. He needs to win and so he learns to assiduously avoid anything he can't do easily. What an order!

The other two life positions are variations on this same theme. In the second one, the child unconsciously decides to eschew attempts to please significant attachment figures after trying and discovering that it simply doesn't work. Instead, he decides to pursue a *Dominant Goal* to the exclusion of affectional relationships with the unconscious belief that he will finally be worthy of parental love and approval when he has earned it by being rich enough, famous enough, esteemed enough. (Arieti/Bemporad, 1978, p. 26-28)

In the third position, the child in a sense "gives up" and opts for a lifetime of dependency on parents or parental substitutes. In exchange for the *self*, the individual expects safety, security and to be passively done for. Although all three life positions reflect a failure to emancipate from the family of origin, this life position is the most extreme and appears on first appraisal to be the most pathological until one looks behind the deceptively successful masks of the obedient and hard-striving adults of positions one and two. For each of these, "What had been lost is an environmental prop that allows the perpetuation of a needed state of self. The depressive does not appear to grieve for the other; rather, he grieves for himself — for being deprived of what the other had supplied." (Arieti/Bomporad, 1978, p. 158) He grieves for himself, for it is he for whom the bell tolls and for his lost sense of well being.

Lastly, the authors will close this chapter with an issue which evokes controversy in both the psychiatric and alcoholism treatment fields regarding the etiology and treatment of depression. The controversy revolves around whether depression is a consequence of loss, a consequence of disordered neurochemistry, or a consequence of an habitually pessimistic and disordered way of viewing the world. What is called in psychiatry the "catacholamine hypothesis" postulates that stress, either acute or chronic, can lead to a depletion in certain neurohumoral transmitters in the central nervous system, specifically norepinephrine and dopamine. The brain is a complex electrochemical system which requires a delicate balance of these transmitters to function properly, and a depletion in crucial central nervous system chemicals alters the behavioral substrata which in turn effects mood states. A depletion in norepinephrine and dopamine can generate a disordered mood state characterized by pessimism, despair, and feelings of helplessness and hopelessness. In addition, the individual so affected may experience sleep disturbance, loss of appetite, weight loss, apathy, and a general loss of pleasure and motivation. If such a disordered mood state persists without alteration for a sufficient length of time, the individual's cognitive processes will come to be characterized by what Aaron Beck calls the "cognitive triad":

1. Negative expectations of the environment
2. Negative view of one's self
3. Negative expectations of the future

(Beck, 1979, P. 11-12)

One explanatory model suggests that a vulnerable individual first experiences a loss, the emotional response to which lasts long enough to lead, to a state of neurohumoral depletion. If at this point there is no appropriate therapeutic intervention, the third step may be the development of a habitually negative self, life, and future view which can persist long after the neurochemical imbalance has righted itself. Hence, individuals who develop seriously disordered mood states may require a number of levels of intervention including supportive psychotherapy, antidepressant medication, and cognitive behavioral alteration of the "cognitive triad." This particular issue evokes controversy because it taps into the treatment biases and turf definitions of the various professions which provide treatment. Among the adherents of the "psychotherapy only" group, there is the belief of "no pain, no gain," and a corollary belief that *real* recovery is unaided by *drugs* and accomplished only by "walking through the pain." Among the cognitive/behavioralists, there is a belief that looking for *underlying causes* of disordered mood is a frivolous exercise in psychological archeology and the royal road to repair lies in teaching the patient to *think right*. Last but not least, are the adherents of neurochemical remedies who believe that the patient only needs to repair his faulty neurochemistry by the addition of amine synaptic transmitters which have been depleted to be restored to normal functioning — no psychotherapy needed, no courses in *right thinking* needed; instead, "relief is just a swallow away."

The authors believe that all three points of view have merit. It has been our experience that a very high percentage of Adult Children whom we have treated have chronic underlying organic or neurochemical depressions, and since this has been how they have always felt, they define their affective state as *normal* in the absence of experience with a non-depressed mood. Antidepressant medication, appropriately prescribed to a non-substance abusing patient in the context of supportive psychotherapy, can help these individuals move from emotional sub-basement eleven to the ground floor and facilitates the release of psychic energy in order to work through their unfinished emotional business. It is at this point in treatment that cognitive behavioral approaches become quite useful in helping to dismantle a life-long habit of viewing the self, the world, and the future in a negative, self-limiting way.

The authors will close this chapter with the following comments by John Bowlby:

"It is important to realize that to attribute a major role in the aetiology of depressive disorders to psychosocial events and in particular to separation and loss, does not preclude attributing a significant role also to neurophysiological processes. That there is a relationship between abnormal levels of certain neuroendocrines and neurotransmitters on the one hand, and affective states and disorders, on the other, is now fairly certain. . . Cognitive and affective states of anxiety and depression, induced in adults by events such as separation and loss, may not only be accompanied by significant changes in the levels of certain neuroendocrines but that these changes are similar to those known often to be present in adults suffering from depression. That often comparable changes can occur also in children who are subjected to separation and loss seems probable. Once brought about, these neuroendocrinological changes may then prolong or intensify the depressive reaction. . . Thus it is conceivable that the state of the neuroendocrine system of individuals who are subjected to severely stressing conditions during childhood might be permanently changed so it becomes thereafter either more sensitive or less so." (Bowlby, 1980, Pp. 261-262)

Chapter Four

# "A Cognitive Life Raft"

It may be surprising to the reader, given the past pages describing the trauma suffered by children growing up in addicted homes, that it is our experience that, by far, the majority of these children do not leave home until the age of eighteen and sometimes later. Even at eighteen, leaving home is frequently more a turn of phrase or a geographical change than actually leaving. The loyalty in these families is tremendous, as is the enmeshment. It is not surprising that the provocative "radical momectomies" practiced by some family therapists in the mid-sixties and seventies did not prove effective with Children of Alcoholics. It is difficult to leave a parent at the age of emancipation if the part of the self so depended on for validation of *being* is left behind, or if the self so tenuously developed depends for its existence on taking care of parents or other children in the family; if caretaking, pleasing, or adjusting to chaos is the only self that is known or has been allowed expression. The roles that were developed in these families to survive the trauma and preserve the self become so merged that leaving home becomes merely a figure of speech.

This does not mean that children in addicted families do not attempt separation at a normal age. Many, in fact, talk about leaving as something that was planned as early as age eight or ten, something not usually thought of by most children at that chronological or developmental age. One Adult Child, who reported that she began to work at the age of ten, spent half of her earnings on her alcoholic parents and kept the other half as savings which she secretly put in the bank and referred to in her childhood diary as her "get-away money." That stash she kept so carefully hidden was considered by her a "ticket to freedom" — a life raft kept for eight years. She said, "Whenever the chaos became too much, I would sneak up to my room and unlock my dream box where I kept magazine articles with pictures of normal families and the kids I thought would be mine someday and where I kept my bank book with growing funds. It was my life raft during those depressing days."

She did leave home at the age of eighteen and went to college, despite her parents' objections to higher education, with the money she had saved. Like so many Adult Children we have seen, she not only left home, but moved three thousand miles away *just in case*. But, three thousand miles away when she was sitting on the bed alone in her dorm room — her first night on the college campus — she felt a familiar anxiety return. She felt helpless, afraid, terrified that something was going to happen . . . the same failure that had been so familiar all those years. She began calling home every other night. She said that soon the awful past memories of home became replaced by a fantasy of an ideal home and childhood. She said that she soon realized she was a failure after all; straight A's weren't good enough, accolades from teacher didn't do it, and neither did being president of the dorm.

She said, "I began to feel, I guess as I always had, that there was something dreadfully wrong with me, that I was crazy —really crazy. I'd stand by the wall at school dances, terrified, not knowing what to say or what to do. I'd watch the other kids there talking so easily, building relationships, and I couldn't — just couldn't. Then I joined the crisis drug squad in the evenings instead. I'd go out on calls to kids that were having bad trips. I always knew what to do. I started going with one of the boys I took care of on a bad trip. I dated him, married him, and then the anxiety for the most part went away. I took care of him and it wasn't until years later that I realized that I had brought the *elephant* of addiction home with me. He never stopped using drugs.''

Many Children of Alcoholics leave home only to search out new relationships that are just like the ones they left behind. Some attempt leaving home, feel *failure* in the outside world and return home feeling like the *crazy ones* they always feared they really were. In many families, more than one Adult Child is living back at home after attempts at moving away. When asked why they moved back home, they focus on their subjective failure at school or in jobs and want to focus on that failure in treatment. When asked, ''What do you think would happen if you and your sisters or brothers moved out of the home?'' First comes surprise at the question, then a request to repeat the question. ''What do you think it would be like for your parents if they were alone at home together?'' Then comes long silence and then the fears: ''They'd divorce?'' ''Dad would beat Mom.'' ''They'd die.'' ''They'd go crazy.'' One Adult Child responded, ''My dad would lose his job, my mom would go crazy, the outside world would invade them if we weren't there to protect them.'' For these children, loyalty to the home is a life or death matter and even geographical moves feel like an impossibility. For them, the thought of never leaving home is not thought of as protecting their parents, but rather, thought of as their own failure. These children not only felt little psychological separation from parents growing up but little physical separation, often feeling like the safety barrier between the parents almost from the time of conception.

Often these kids were told they were the reason the parents stayed together or they became the buffers in violence. Some became the pseudo partner to one or both parents and were covertly or overtly sexually abused from an early age. These kids grew up with their psychological and physical boundaries violated regularly and as a result were frequently violated by others as adults, or they abusively violated others, never knowing why. It never occurred to them until receiving education in groups or therapy that they never understood boundaries and privacy. They had been violated as children and consequently never developed the concept of themselves as separate individuals. They had difficulty recognizing where they stopped and others began, both psychologically and physically. Love meant giving oneself away.

If a child has never been able to develop a sense of self in a family, then leaving home at the age of emancipation becomes no more than a cardboard fantasy. Many Adult Children as kids built their hopes and dreams of freedom and future life on television shows like *Leave It To Beaver*, *Ozzie and Harriet*, *The Waltons*, or *Cinderella*. They believed, because they had to believe in order to survive, that *normal* would magically fall into place once they passed beyond the doorstep of their alcoholic family. But television characters are not good models and cannot provide the necessary nurturing to a child to allow the development of a self. Once the process of true grief has been completed, the traumas walked through, and the child inside allowed growth and integration, those TV characters appear to be poor imitations of real life. They find that the characters against whom they have judged themselves as normal or crazy were not in the least representative of the ups and downs, joys and sorrows, healthy conflicts, fears and peace of normal life. They were only validations of images, not real human beings.

### Caged Tears

My stomach turns at the thought
Of the abuse to a little tot

She was tiny  She was fair
All she wanted was loving care

Touch me    Touch me    The baby cried
They would not    So she died

*She was finally raised from the crib*

*But bears the scars*

*Parents love you    Do they not*

*Think again my little tot*

*All the tears your crib has caged*

*Cry for baby sorely aged*

*Cry for baby's pent-up rage*

**by Jo Kelly**

Frequently in workshops or in individual therapy we ask Adult Children to do continuum of life drawings such as those represented on the following two pages. They draw early years, adult years, and years projected into the future. Frequently, the drawings that depict age eighteen are birds flying away or paths leading to mountains, suns or rainbows, and have little human life depicted. The drawings that depict age twenty-one (next in sequence) are black clouds, tears, or drug and alcohol, reflecting the pain or the addiction to the realization that the fantasy of freedom or of *normal* didn't just magically appear after physical emancipation from the childhood home.

One Adult Child who had drawn a picture of a world exploding in her twenty-first years said, "I don't know if other kids read existential writers like Kafka or Camus when they were young, but I did. Somehow I guess I was trying to find the meaning in my life and the struggles in their novels appealed to me — you know, like a person waking up one morning and finding that they had turned into a bug for no reason, or a man put on trial and convicted and sentenced without ever knowing what crime he'd committed. It felt like my life. When I was fifteen, I wrote a paper for class entitled *Franz Kafka —Blindman or Prophet?* At age twenty-one, after I realized that all those fantasies of adult life I dwelled on as a kid were never going to come true, I knew he was a prophet. I didn't feel that anything I could do could change how miserable I felt or the fact that I had

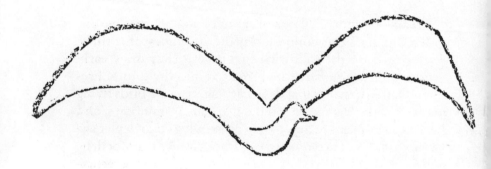

no idea what normal was. I felt as helpless and confused as that man who had been turned into a bug and realized that becoming a 'free' adult didn't make any difference. I felt my parents were right all along; my dreams had been worthless; I was the crazy one and I found myself drinking just like they did."

Leave It To Beaver or books by writers like Franz Kafka or Albert Camus are only temporary life rafts for children who grow up in alcoholic families. Much stronger life rafts are needed if an Adult Child is to feel safe diving into the emotional waters to find the true self which was left behind. It is important for the Adult Child to have the safety of a trusting relationship (discussed in Chapter Seven) and the cognitive life raft created by understanding, on an intellectual level, what growing up in an alcoholic or addicted family meant in terms of psychological development. Allowing expression to that child of the past that experienced the trauma and developing compassion, rather than contempt for that child, is the essence of the grief work process. Walking through the trauma, feeling the pain, the tears, the fears never expressed is often a frightening process, but a necessary one if an Adult Child is to move beyond survival to the spontaneity of living her/his life rather than being locked in the prison of an *ideal* constructed by parents who never cried their own tears or achieved emotional freedom.

A "cognitive life raft" in order to intellectually understand the beginning, the middle, and the end of the process is a type of security that can relieve, to some extent, the terrifying anxiety of *not knowing* or feeling *crazy* when emotions begin to surface. This *life raft* of understanding is much like reading the last page of a novel that has rendered its reader panicked in the middle. When one knows the ending, it often allows a sense of control in the frightening middle. Adult Children need a sense of safety that was never there and a belief that those feelings held inside for so long are not as powerful as they have believed them to be. They need to feel that the expression of feelings is safe within the structure of a new relationship where trust has been built, unlike the relationships in childhood which condemned their expression.

Perhaps the most important part of the *cognitive life raft* for Adult Children is that it *normalizes* the struggle. It is important for them to understand that they are not *crazy* as they have always feared, but instead are suffering the complications of delayed grief and, frequently, multigenerational delayed grief. For many, alcoholism or addiction in their families spans three or more generations and with the addiction, generations of lost childhoods, deaths from alcoholism, suicides, divorces, medical complications, misdiagnosed nervous breakdowns, emotional detachment and losses too numerous to mention, as well as for some, the effects of financial collapse, world wars, and immigration.

About six years ago, we began doing workshops for Adult Children of alcoholics. The workshops began as trainings for professionals on the effects of growing up in addicted families. At the time we began the workshops, it was our belief that the reason why alcoholism and drug abuse was frequently missed by human service professionals was that a large majority of those professionals were themselves children from addicted families still caught in denial. While doing professional training regarding alcoholism, addiction, and depression we had also found that many in the audience would come up to us during the break and whisper, "I grew up in an alcoholic family, but have never found a safe place to discuss it."

We found during our first workshop that we were correct, and that 95% of the professionals that came were from alcoholic homes. They didn't want training, per se, but rather information, a cognitive life raft, and a safe place to talk about what it meant to them to have grown up in addicted families. We have done a workshop every two months since that time and exceed the 60-person limit each time, leaving a waiting list for the next workshop. The participants tell us after hearing the characteristics of alcoholic and addicted family systems and the roles and characteristics of Adult Children that for the first time in their lives they don't feel crazy but instead feel like survivors of trauma — victims of victims. They feel less unique, more connected with others, and more hopeful about their lives and the lives of their families, believing that generational grief can end here with some work, and that the unexplainable internal chaos and depression that they have felt all of their lives does not have to be passed down to their children.

Many of the participants have themselves been alcoholic or drug-addicted, most are in recovery, some just beginning recovery or seeing for the first time their own drinking or drug-abuse patterns. Many have never drunk and have been terrified all their lives of taking even a sip of alcohol or even using pain medications for surgery. Some are children of Adult Children and feel the effects of the grandparents' addictions on their own parents. None are insensitive to the effects of alcohol. Most participants are able for the first time in their lives to acknowledge the elephant in the living room that they had never been allowed to say they saw, and how that elephant, which sometimes was funny and pleasant, had also caused so much pain. Others in the workshop, by speaking of their own experiences, validated the feelings, experiences, and memories of fellow participants, many expressing as one woman did, "I still feel the pain and I know I have a long way to go, but for the first time in my life I feel a sense of being normal instead of crazy." Some leave feeling a sense of awkwardness and fear concerning breaking the long-standing loyalty in the family of never talking about what it was really like. One or two individuals over the years have come to the workshop several times, first standing outside the door all day, listening, afraid to come in even though parents may live three thousand miles away, afraid that they will be seen breaking the family loyalty. Then they come in, but can't manage to talk at first, still feeling the fear. One day they talk about what it was like for that child and validate the child for the first time saying timidly, "I grew up in an alcoholic family."

Some Adult Children spend the day at the workshop feeling at first a sense of confusion, doing what Adult Children do so well — minimizing the effects of their alcoholic families, minimizing the child's experience, thinking or saying, "Maybe

I didn't have it so bad. Maybe my parents weren't really alcoholic. There was no violence in my family and no abuse. My parents drank every night, but they never raised their voices." Others validate their unspoken words, "Mine didn't either, but they weren't there for us. Can we really compare whose pain was worse? That's what I've been doing all my life. I almost feel it was harder for us because there were no signs of abuse outwardly. I just felt crazy because the outside looked good, but I still felt the constant abandonment."

During the day-long workshop, participants learn what normal was in their alcoholic families. They learn most of all that "people who lean on people who lean on bottles fall over," and that the focus in an alcoholic family is on an addiction rather than on the developing needs of children. They also learn that not just the alcoholic, but all members of the addicted family live in denial, and they learn about the extreme insecurity and inconsistency that leads to the development of denial and the resulting roles needed to survive.

Participants are shown the characteristics of children who grow up in addicted families: shame, guilt, perfectionism, counterdependence (defensive self-reliance), the need to control, the need to be right, addictions to chaos, workaholism, black and white thinking, chronic overachievement or fear of success, inability to relax and let go and have fun, or constant depression and anxiety. After seeing these characteristics, they tell us that for the first time they feel like someone else was there, that they are not alone or so terrifyingly unique, and that perhaps they aren't crazy after all.

As they listen to others talk about their own relationship addictions, illnesses, constant insecurities, compulsions regarding food, panic attacks, or substance-abuse histories, they realize the price Children of Alcoholics pay for that survival adaption. Many feel, as one woman said, "It's almost like I've finally found that safe home, that place where I can finally begin to let others and myself know who 'me' is. It has been so exhausting and lonely pretending all these years and yet never knowing why. I've worked so hard to be perfect and yet I never believed the A's. Now I know why. How could I believe them? I've always felt like that *competent imposter* that would some day be found out."

Those participants that were survivors of sexual abuse in their alcoholic families learned that they too were not so unique, and feel enough validation — some for the first time in their lives — to tell the secret that has been eating them up figuratively and literally since early childhood. They begin to understand their confusion of affection and sexuality, their sense of feeling always like objects, their secretive compulsive lies, their sexual identity confusion, and their poor sense of boundaries as the result of pervasive boundary violation as children, rather than the result of craziness they have always feared.

Most of all, they learn that it is possible to feel nurtured and abused at the same time and that the abuse wasn't their fault. They begin to get a sense, if only vaguely, of how small they were, how young they were. Participants who were abused physically or sexually begin to make intellectual sense out of their pervasive fear of normal conflict, their fear of trusting, and the patterns of repetitive abuse in their adult lives. Even though the *cognitive life raft* does not ease the pain or the fear of trust, participants report a lessening of pervasive shame. They begin to realize, if only intellectually, that with work their lives can change and that perhaps someday that rigid control they feel as such a prison can lessen and they can feel and enjoy the spontaneity others seem to have achieved.

One participant told a story in a workshop that could be a metaphor for the feelings held by many Adult Children: "A year or so ago, I was skiing with some friends when I lost control and fell down a steep embankment. I lay there for some time and then I could see the ski patrol starting to come down the hill to rescue me. I looked down at my leg that was split open and bleeding and felt an overwhelming sense of embarrassment and protection for those on the ski patrol. I yelled up at them, 'You'd better not come down here right now; it's a mess down here.' "

Most Adult Children report that all their lives they have felt that they were "a mess deep down" and have protected themselves and others from the embarrassment of seeing or feeling that "mess" they felt they were. They have felt alone in a crowd, or isolated themselves all their lives. They have taken care of others compulsively, but never let others care for them and have sought out relationships where needs weren't possible or intimacy could never be achieved. Children of Alcoholics tend to have caseloads, not friends, and feel that they have to work harder than anyone else, be more perfect, or tough, or independent to hide the craziness they feel inside or to earn their right to live in the world like everyone else. The workshops, the education, the *cognitive life raft* are not ends in themselves, but the beginning of a process, a validation, a normalizing that allows Adult Children to feel a little less lonely, a little less afraid of the feelings inside, a little less ashamed of that family they protected. There are ways of welcoming that small child, so long locked in the prison of the ideal self, to the planet earth where the feelings of fear, anger, joy, sadness, and normal anxiety are seen, first intellectually, then with work, emotionally, as not bad, dangerous, or crazy, but rather as part of what it means to just be human.

After the workshop, most Adult Children seek out a safe therapeutic relationship, an emotional net where they can begin the process of griefwork. Many participants in our workshops have been in therapy before and have either been given tranquilizers or other medications for emotions they felt were *out of control*, or else worked for years in therapy on behavior change, never having touched the child inside or dealt with the abandonment or the abuse experienced in their alcoholic family. They had their emotions treated as symptoms of something else, never had their own substance-abuse patterns confronted, or left therapy after a short time because their therapist only saw what they projected — a self that looked so good, so competent, so together. They never even started to form a trusting therapeutic relationship or begin the process of grief.

Prior to the Adult Children's Movement, which began about 1979, few therapists understood the concept of delayed grief in alcoholic families and Adult Children were diagnosed as having everything from "manic depressive illness" to "adjustment reactions." An "adjustment reaction" is an "abnormal response to a normal life situation." (DSM III) Dr. Timmen Cermack, the first president of the National Organization For Children of Alcoholics, was instrumental in changing that diagnosis to "delayed stress syndrome" (Cermack, 1984). "Delayed stress syndrome" is a "normal response to an abnormal life situation." (DSM III) Growing up in an alcoholic family is definitely not normal.

The symptoms displayed by Adult Children are similar to those shown by other trauma victims or veterans of war and the treatment is also the same — the necessity to walk back through the trauma over and over again with a trusted other. The first step is that *cognitive life raft*. The second step is an ending of denial of past experience and sometimes current substance-abuse patterns. It is our feeling that intensive work on grief cannot take place until an individual has experienced at least a year of abstinence and sobriety. One cannot grieve while still toxic. The third step is forming a trusting relationship with a therapist, establishing that *emotional net*. The fourth step is the process of grief. The fifth step is integration of parents and true self, and the sixth step, which follows automatically after the tears, is behavior change.

Before working through the grief, attempts at changing behavior become only more expectations of an ideal self. If we had a nickel for every Adult Child who had spent endless amounts of money on behavioral training, self-help books and workbooks designed to help them be more assertive, have more self-esteem, learn to express anger, or work out conflicts in marriage, we would be wealthy people. Adult Children who have taken classes designed to change behavior without working through the feelings of the frightened child that lives inside, not only have difficulty following through with expected changes, but add these new failures to those other feelings of failure stored long ago.

One woman stated, "I felt like a failure every time I couldn't say 'no' or couldn't stand up for myself. It only convinced me more that I was as *crazy* as I always thought myself to be. I felt even more helpless; only this time, I saw the instructor as that punitive parent who would look at me as a failure, so I began to lie about what I could do. I felt even worse."

With the *cognitive life raft* comes validation on an intellectual level of the feelings of the child and a *normalizing* of responses that always felt uniquely crazy. The increased public awareness of what it means to grow up in an alcoholic family has begun the process of providing that education and is now allowing children of addicted families to believe that things can change after the tears.

*It was to be an experiment.*

*A role play between myself and mother.*

*To bring forth feelings from the past.*

*That part of me that seeks recovery was eager.*

*The lost child was*

   *terrified.*

*I sat,*

*staring at the empty chair.*

*A faraway voice urged me to speak.*

*My mother's image sat primly across.*

*The familiar smirk on her face.*

*The one that says*

*"You are worthless; your feelings unimportant."*

*Her body, slender and hard,*

*emitting an aura of*

*"What you have to say had better be important*

*and worth wasting my valuable time."*

*Her hair short and silver,*

*beauty shop perfect,*

*Benjamin Franklin glasses perched on her nose.*

*All business now,*
*her defenses so well fortified*
*that nothing could ever*
*penetrate her wall.*

*It was as if someone else was sitting in my chair.*
*Perhaps, the small frightened child within me.*
*The one who knows no safe places, no boundaries.*
*Who has been intruded upon countless times.*

*At first, the child was silent.*
*Tears streamed down her face.*
*Shaking, sobbing, and petrified,*
*that her mother would reject her once again.*
*That one more time it would somehow be her fault.*

*The little girl rocked to and fro,*
*hugging herself, grieving.*
*Remembering all the times*
*she sat in her darkened room,*
*alone and confused.*

*Wishing, praying*
*that she was in reality*
*a gypsy princess*
*who had been mistakenly left*
*with this family.*
*Creating fantasy and fairy tales*
*to make reality*
*bearable.*

*— **Nanci Presley-Holley***

*The little girl couldn't trust*
*her mother to protect her.*
*Nor hold her when frightened.*
*Or listen when she was a success.*
*Or validate*
*her anger,*
*her joy.*

*The child was to be totally emotionless.*
*A passive, unobtrusive mask for all who passed before her.*
*Knowing how to care for herself*
*through some inborn knowledge.*
*And most importantly to be silent*
*and oh, so very good.*

*Anger spewed forth.*
*The child wanted to kick and bite*
*the granite wall that mother hid behind.*
*Screaming,*
*"How could you do this to me?*
*Why did you hate me?*
*Was it because I looked like my father?*
*Was I ugly?*
*Or because I was too fat?*
*Too thin?*
*Or because I was a girl?*
*Or because I was?"*

*The whole incident*
*took less than 10 minutes,*
*but it was an eternity for the child.*
*She had been waiting a lifetime.*

*There was no critical parent*
*to berate and invalidate her feelings.*
*She was allowed to feel and be.*

*I awoke as if from a dream.*
*A calmness spreading within.*
*I began to understand what had been said*
*that underlying my anger, my resentments*
  *was fear.*
*Fear of abandonment,*
*fear of success,*
*fear of losing again.*

*This loving parent I am creating,*
*took the child in her arms and said,*
*"You are perfect.*
*God's creation.*
*An integral part of my life.*
*You exist."*

— **Nanci Presley-Holley**
*9/13/85*

**Chapter Five**

# An Emotional Net: Building a Relationship With The Child Within

"I don't know why I'm here. I feel a bit foolish. I know that when you asked me what the problem is, I really won't know," Beth said, looking embarrassed, although trying to appear confident. It was the same type of relaxed appearance that I had seen so many times before. She had a smile on her face and her hands were folded in her lap, but her posture told me that if I pulled the chair out from under her she wouldn't move, but instead would assume the same *relaxed* position in mid-air. The message that she had left on my answering machine a few weeks earlier was also familiar, "I was at your workshop last week and it affected me a great deal. I don't know why I'm calling. I know you're busy working with people who need your time far more than I. I'd like to make an appointment if you have time. If you don't, I will understand."

At the beginning of our first appointment, I explained to Beth that this first session was a time for both of us to decide whether or not we would continue working together. I also explained that it was often a difficult process to begin and that I didn't expect her to trust me too soon. With that explanation, she relaxed a bit. I asked many questions regarding her history; use of chemicals; past and present, what it was like growing up in her family; birthdays; special times; and history of losses. I asked whether she had been physically or sexually abused as a child; about her past therapy experiences and history of relationships, and about depression and eating disorders. Beth told me that she had been in therapy twice before, once when a marriage had failed. On this occasion she had been prescribed tranquilizers. The second time was when her mother died. "I was in therapy briefly when my mother died. I was so depressed and I had to keep functioning. I only went for six or seven sessions. I thought I felt better. At first I was given medications to help me sleep, but I was afraid to take them. We didn't talk about my alcoholic family though and I didn't realize then that it had affected me. We didn't talk a lot about my mother or dad. The therapist just told me that the death of someone close was difficult and we worked on how it was affecting my daily life. It wasn't really, I mean, I still went to work everyday. I always have. I made all the funeral arrangements and just kept going. Anyway, he said my reaction was normal and I didn't need to come back if I didn't want to. He was a busy man and I was all right. I just kept feeling the loneliness I always have."

In the last several years, we have heard many stories similar to Beth's regarding experiences in therapy, either repetitive short periods of therapy with little change on a feeling level (intervention that focused on behavior rather than the massive amounts of grief beneath the behavior), or focus on symptom relief with intermittent uses of tranquilizers or anti-anxiety agents, without related therapeutic work on the effects of growing up in an alcoholic home. In those cases, the adults, like Beth, never dealt with the underlying problems of felt abandonment, boundary violations, early trauma, delayed development or physical or sexual abuse histories. Many never told the therapist about early abuse, significant lifelong depressions, long-term eating disorders or substance abuse, "because they were never asked." Others were terminated from therapy because the therapist only saw the projected ideal image and wondered why the client was even in treatment. Many spent years in therapy focusing on issues in the present and continued to use drugs or alcohol throughout the process.

As stated earlier, delayed grief wears many masks, and the terror of being *crazy* (many Adult Children have secretly felt this way all of their lives) is often inadvertently validated in therapy, rather than validation of the frightened child locked so deeply within. In order to have access to that child and to feel safe enough to walk back through the traumas, there must be a feeling of trust of self and the trust of at least one significant other with whom to work through the process — a type of emotional net that was never there in childhood. The longest part of this process is not the grief work itself, but the forming of a trusting relationship that eventually leads to the Adult Child's acceptance and validation of the child they once were.

To describe this process, let's turn to the story of Joan. As the reader may recall, the self-portrait Joan drew so creatively in therapy contained three different parts of herself which she perceived herself to be: the ballerina (her ideal image); the woman with the knife (lifelong depression); and the frightened tiny child (representing her true self locked within). She also answered, when asked, which part she thought was the strongest, "It must be the ballerina or the woman with the knife, because I've been trying to get rid of that fearful kid all my life." If Joan had gone to a therapist or a group that paid attention only to her reality problem, i.e., the fact that she had injured her knee and couldn't dance, the therapist would have perhaps focused on her need to productively re-enter the work force or ways in which she could re-engage with the community and friends. If the focus had been on her depression of suicidal ideation, perhaps she would have been unnecessarily medicated, hospitalized, or primarily focused on her anger regarding the injury. In either case, the attention given to the child within and the early trauma to that child might have taken a back seat to the woman with the knife or the ballerina ideal.

In Joan's case, the framework for her therapy process was set in the first two sessions. In the first session, significant history was gathered, not only of her presenting depression, but also of her years growing up in an alcoholic family, how she perceived herself in the family, and her significant history of losses. She was also asked questions regarding her history of chemical use, to which she replied, "I have a drink once in a while, it used to be one or two glasses of wine at dinner and perhaps a drink or two following a performance. Lately, I've had more alone-time and have found my drinking increased a bit. I don't think it's a problem though." She also stated that she smoked marijuana occasionally to relax a bit or while she was writing. It was explained to Joan that drinking or the use of mind-altering chemicals would not be allowed during the treatment process. Her response was, "But I don't have a problem with chemicals." And the response that followed was "Then you probably won't have difficulty giving it up during treatment." It was also explained that the major work that she would be undertaking was grief work and that the use of chemicals would interfere in that process and that the work we did together would be of little benefit to her if she continued even occasional use. We also discussed the depressive effects of chemical use. It was explained to Joan that grief work was not a short-term process and that it would probably take time for her to trust enough to allow herself to grieve.

It has been our experience that a successful grief work and mourning process with Adult Children in individual group therapy or psychodramatic therapy is a five-step process: 1) Breaking Through Denial; 2) Building a Cognitive Life Raft; 3) Building a Relationship (An Emotional Net); 4) Grief Work (Walking Back Through Trauma); and 5) Mourning and Integration.

### Breaking Through Denial

It is not surprising, given the discussions on trauma and development in the First and Second Chapters, that denial is the hallmark of the alcoholic family. Years ago when denial was discussed in relation to alcoholism, the focus was on the denial of the alcoholic only. Even at that, it was difficult for some counselors to understand the difference between denial and lying. It was common in treatment centers in the early 1960s to hear novice counselors or family members leave a confrontation with an alcoholic in frustration saying, "Why does this person lie about her/his drinking? He/she just got a DWI and is still telling us there is no problem. Does he/she think we're stupid or blind?" It is just now becoming understood that alcoholism is the disease of denial, and that many of the behaviors that surround this denial, e.g., constructing events out of blackouts; hiding bottles; convincing the boss one more time that it was really the flu; telling elaborate stories about sitting in a bar all afternoon without taking a drink (that being used as proof that the person has no problem with alcohol); are not attempts to fool or lie to others, but attempts to convince the self that everything is OK. Yet, along with the alcoholic himself, denial is still protected by many; some doctors still refuse to call the disease process caused by drinking by its proper name: The Disease of Alcoholism. Some policemen still don't arrest a woman and issue a DWI because "she's a nice lady with a nice husband," and some counselors still allow their clients to drink throughout their therapy, focusing energy on depression or phobias instead of the underlying alcoholism.

With family members, denial is even less well-understood. One constantly hears the question: "Why does that nice person put up with the drinking of his/her partner?" "Why don't they leave or set limits?" "How can he talk about how proud his father is of his athletic achievements when he never comes to a game?" or "How did she get voted 'happiest in her high school class' with two alcoholic parents?" The questions could be answered with two other questions. "If family members really acknowledge the effects of living with an alcoholic, what else would have to be acknowledged and felt?" "If an Adult Child allowed recognition of the depth of loss and abandonment felt in the realization that parents were not always there, or felt the trauma of driving a car at age seven, what would that do to the fantasy parents still depended on for nurturing, validation of the fantasy self (ideal image) and survival."

Denial is part of the fabric of all of our lives and yet is possibly one of the least understood of all survival mechanisms. Most of us experience it nightly when watching the news. When we hear the statistics that a thousand people were killed in some way somewhere, we don't put faces on those bodies; we reduce it all to a statistic or stop watching the news. When we hear that a hurricane hit a few hundred miles away killing one hundred people, we convince ourselves that it would never happen in our area. If we hear that a plane crashed somewhere last night killing three hundred people and we have to fly the next day, we convince ourselves that it would never happen to "this" plane. We deny our own vulnerability, or medicate ourselves by drinking throughout the flight. We become numb to what is really being said, eliminate it from our minds, or distract ourselves with happier news. If we, at a young age, had parents die in a plane crash, what would we do to convince ourselves that we weren't really alone. What would make it possible for us to get on a similar plane ten years later? Some children, without support, would focus on the plane rather than the loss and never ride in a plane again or would panic whenever they passed an airport and perhaps never know why. Some would become pilots or flight attendants in order to prove to themselves their own power and strength over vulnerability rather than face the helplessness of loss. Some would become engineers specializing in plane repair, becoming driven with attaining new skill in the area and yet never really comprehend why they chose such a profession.

If these children had a strong support system of other caring adults, they would eventually feel the anger at being abandoned so young, feel the pain and sadness at never seeing mommy or daddy again, vent anger at planes, at mom and dad for dying, at God, and at life and its unfairness. They would work through the tragedy in play over and over again, integrating the feelings and the event rather than repressing them.

They would attach to the new adult figures in their lives while always keeping the positive memories in their hearts of mom and dad. They would perhaps cry occasionally as adults when they heard the news of a plane crash, and they would know why and perhaps look at pictures kept of mom and dad stored in a special place, but their lives wouldn't be driven by the avoidance of, or power over air flight. They wouldn't need to marry or become a pilot or avoid forming relationships. They wouldn't fly into a rage when they saw their ten-year-old child playing with a model airplane because of the repressed feelings it stimulated in them. They wouldn't fill their children's room with pictures of planes, convincing them to be pilots and making their children tough, so they could remain tough.

When Joan and Richard first came into treatment, they had some realization of internal pain and problems in their lives. For Joan, it was severe depression originally stimulated by an injury that limited her career as a dancer. For Richard, it was the recognition that he had become powerless over his drinking. Joan's original focus was on her loss of dance with little realization of why the loss of a career would take away her reason for living. She had little idea of why she had chosen dance as a career and why her career had literally become the total focus of her life. Richard's focus was originally on a feared relapse after a year of sobriety. He had little idea of why he didn't have the belief that he could succeed in sobriety or other things he attempted in his life; why he believed so strongly that he wasn't a man if he didn't drink; or why he constantly had nightmares that showed failure and trauma around every corner.

Breaking through denial for each of them wasn't just the process of acknowledging difficulty in their current lives, but also acknowledging the existence of a frightened child within. One Adult Child stated that he really began the grief process in therapy when he imagined a visual picture of a tiny child within himself who had been contained in a block of ice all of his life. "I felt a part of me was frozen." At that moment he didn't feel the pain of the child inside him or have clear memories of the traumas he went through as a child. He just had a feeling of a frozen state inside. Memories later emerged during the grief process, but for the first time he acknowledged the existence of a part of himself. The process of coming out of denial involves validating the existence of that child, recognizing the effects of living in an alcoholic home, and with the help of the therapist, putting a face on the child within.

Beginning with the first session, the therapist starts the process of giving a face to that child and validating how difficult it was to grow up in an alcoholic home. Any questions regarding the family, such as: who played which roles; was there physical, psychological, or sexual abuse, etc., help the client to understand that the child within did experience what he/she remembers, and probably the pain as well. No matter what the answers are to the questions, this is the process of validation.

The mistake that many Adult Children (and frequently their therapists) make in the treatment process, is to believe that because the adult feels little trauma or remembers little about her/his childhood, it means that the child inside is not in pain or suffering from delayed grief. Many Adult Children will say, "When you talk about the characteristics of an alcoholic home, I feel a sadness inside, but I don't know why because my childhood wasn't that painful." A therapist might say, "I treated Joe for a long time, but after a while it didn't seem like we were going anywhere. He was feeling better and things were going well in his life so it seemed like he had completed his work." When such statements are made, we have forgotten about that *frozen child* and how that child became encased in ice in the first place.

Let's imagine observing a little five-year-old girl on her way to kindergarten for the first time. She is timid and tearful, frightened and excited. We see her leaving the door of her house and she's begging her mother to come with her and crying and saying she's afraid. Her mother becomes more and more frustrated and tells the little girl, "You're acting like a baby. You're a big girl now and big girls don't cry and they don't need their mothers to take them to school." The little girl continues to cry, but appears embarrassed by her tears.

The mother becomes really frustrated and yells, "Can't you see I'm busy with your brother and your dad's sick? You're really making me angry." With that, the mom shuts the door in frustration and the little girl takes a deep breath, dries her eyes and with a determined look begins walking to school. The child was afraid, but the girl walking to school put away her fear, determined to gain her mother's approval and be a big girl.

When this adult is asked in therapy, "Were there times as a child when you were afraid?" The determined woman would say, "Why no." The little child inside however would hear the question, still feel frightened of feeling fear or trusting, and would later in therapy remember the incident and the feelings with it after a trusting connection had been established. This adult might experience some degree of depression in the fall every year but she may never link the original memory with the feelings of depression or anxiety that she is experiencing in her life.

The therapist assists the Adult Child in coming out of denial by asking questions and modeling feelings that were never modeled by parents, e.g., "How did you feel? You must have been frightened all by yourself in a strange new place." By setting limits: "You cannot use drugs or alcohol during the therapy process. I care about you, and alcohol and drugs change feelings just like they did in your family. I will be consistent about that limit," or; by acknowledging boundaries and personal space: "I don't expect you to trust me during the beginning of this process. You are you and I am me. Trust is developed, not demanded. I expect you to be who you are."

In the first few sessions, the therapist might ask the Adult Child to complete a loss history. In both Joan's and Richard's case, this request was originally met with confusion, then an attempt to remember early deaths in the family. It was clarified to each of them that early losses were not only losses of people in their lives, but also losses of childhood experiences, toys, pets, special occasions, nurturing, childhood friends, ability to express particular emotions, innocence, freedoms, or

entire stages of child development. In both cases, the losses
that they originally believed to be quite small were actually
quite large. Each was surprised at the number of losses in early
childhood and teenage years and. were also surprised by the
feelings of sadness or anger that began to emerge during the
process of remembering them. For each, it was the first time
that they began to recognize the impact of growing up in an
alcoholic family. Both Richard and Joan were asked to put the
age of loss by each event or example, along with the time of
year. They were also asked to bring in pictures of themselves at
early ages.

When reviewing the losses experienced, we also look at
their pictures at the age of each loss. Joan remembered with
amazement that she was only five years old when she first
realized that there was no Santa Claus. She had been awakened
at about three o'clock on Christmas morning by her parents
fighting over assembling her younger brother's tricycle. Her
dad was drunk and was lying next to the partially assembled
tricycle with a wrench in his hand, and her mother was
screaming at him while trying to wake him up to complete the
task. She realized that it was on that occasion that she lost the
magic of childhood. She also realized that, even at that age, she
was more preoccupied with the fear that her three-year-old
brother would wake up, than with her own feelings of sadness.
She had gone downstairs to help her crying mother fix the trike
and felt horribly guilty that she couldn't figure out the task.
When we looked at a picture of the five-year-old little Joan,
she said with amazement, "I never realized how small I was. I
was just a little girl." She also said, "I wonder if that is why I feel
so depressed every Christmas?" For Joan, it was the first time
she began to feel empathy for the child inside her, and was the
first time that "fearful kid" had a face. She could not, at that
time, feel what the child felt, cry the tears or feel the anger, but
she could acknowledge for the first time that she had been
affected.

In Richard's case, his first "loss memory" was at the age of
six. It was a Saturday and he was at home alone with his father
who had been drinking heavily since early morning. His

mother was at work. He remembered hearing the screeching of tires outside his house. He ran to the front door to find that his best friend, the family dog, Skippy, had been hit by a car. The dog's hind legs had been broken and he couldn't move. He remembered screaming to his father for help. He remembered his father's words, "How many times have I told you to watch that damn dog?" "How come the dog was in the road?" He remembered standing there when his father shot the dog. He held Skippy in his arms until his mother came home from work, but he didn't remember crying. He and his mother buried the pet in the back yard and he could still hear his mother's words, "Why didn't you take Skippy to the vet?" Richard related the story with little feeling, then replied, "Even at six years old, I couldn't do anything right." I asked him to look at the picture of himself at age six standing next to his father. I asked, "Look how small you were. Who was the adult?" Richard looked surprised. Later in the session, Richard replied, "I don't hate animals, I loved that dog. He was my life back then. I told Skippy everything. He loved me too. I have always fought with my wife about dogs. I'd never let her get one and we'd always fight about it. I thought it was because I hated dogs. I don't. I loved Skippy."

The process of coming out of denial takes many forms with Adult Children. For some, it is the recognition of the frightened child. For some, the sad child and for others, the angry child. In Richard's case, he had far less difficulty expressing his anger than his tears. Anger had become a wall that he lived behind, a fire-breathing dragon that gave him a sense of false protection, yet, at times, would turn on him and spit contempt at the child within. For some Adult Children, coming out of denial also involves the recognition of long-term addictive patterns of drinking, drug abuse, or eating disorders. The group or individual therapist may be the first person in their lives who set consistent limits, thereby offering care, support and a safe structure to the frightened child who lives behind the wall or image. Saying to an individual with a long-term pattern of bulimic behavior, "I will not treat you unless you are also willing to be under a physician's care," is also saying something to the child to whom you are showing care. Your protection of the child is, perhaps, the first experience that child has had of a consistent and protective buffer in the world — a way of saying to the child within: "I care about you."

It is not possible for the Adult Child to come out of denial if the therapist is in her/his own denial. The child has lived her/his life with faulty mirroring. The therapist may become an extension of that faulty mirroring if he/she is afraid to ask questions about, and validate the multitude of feelings that the child experienced (love, fear, anger, sadness, loss) because the therapist has not yet cried her/his own tears about childhood feelings.

## Building a Bridge

In earlier chapters, the authors have discussed the belief that the end result of being raised in an alcoholic family or a family whose major foundations are built on denial is frequently a huge gap between the self and the ideal self or image. The child learns well at an early age that to be who he/she is, to express needs or spontaneous feelings, is to be rendered helpless or orphaned in the family. Those entrusted with the care of the child are not consistently available or nurturing; they often show injury at the expression of the child's true feelings. Often these parents violate the psychological, and sometimes physical boundaries of the child, and are not capable of supplying unconditional love and regard. Sometimes, because of their own need for self-regard and nurturing, they can accept only the mirror image of what they wish and need the child to be. What results is the development of a *looking-glass* self with the child, or true self, encased in ice.

It is not surprising, given this developmental process, that it is not the child that the therapist meets in the early sessions, but rather the *looking-glass* self. Most Adult Children originally come into therapy not because of empathy for themselves or pain at their own childhood losses, but rather to make their image stronger, better looking, more pleasing to others, tougher, or better able to cope with isolation. They want to lose weight; get a better job; get rid of depression so they can have more energy for work or others; figure out what they need to change about themselves to retrieve an isolating or abusive relationship; or to learn from the therapist how to be an even better need satisfying object for partners, parents, or other siblings. They want tools to add to the enormous tool case that they already carry on their backs, more self-help books to be an even more acceptable person, or want the therapist to help in the construction of an even stronger mask that the therapist might validate if they can work to be the *perfect client.* The Adult Children who possess great empathy and care for others in their world, and for the conditions of the world itself, frequently have contempt for the child still encased in ice. We see the Adult Children we meet as individuals like those described by Alice Miller: "They recount their earliest memories without any sympathy for the child they once were, and this is more striking since these patients not only have a pronounced introspective ability, but are also able to empathize well with other people. The relationship to their own childhood emotional world, however, is characterized by lack of respect, compulsion to control, manipulation and a demand for achievement." (Miller, 1981, p. 6)

Part of the role of the therapist, group leader, or psychodramatist, is to, perhaps for the first time, welcome the child to the planet earth; help the adult construct a bridge between the image ideal and the child of earlier days, using the materials from both; provide validation for the frightened child, and for the survivorship of the adult; aid in the construction of internal psychological and physical boundaries; and to become a mirror for the child rather than for the image. Sometimes the therapist may serve as a protective buffer between an internalized abusive parent and the abused child. Sometimes the therapist may help provide the support and map for the child to walk back through the trauma of childhood, while helping the client to feel safe enough to reconnect the memory of the experience with the feelings once repressed, thereby aiding in the release of the child held so long as a hostage.

Part of the survival mechanism of the child raised in an alcoholic family frequently depends on the ability to be aware of parental needs and feelings, and to be able to constantly be observant of changes in parental moods and behavior. The child, therefore, earns a Ph.D. at the age of six in observing the behavior of others and assessing parental needs, but is in elementary school at the age of thirty, trying to learn the ability to assess, label, or communicate her/his own needs and feelings. Because of constant psychological boundary violations as children, these adults make a full-time occupation of *mind reading* with partners, friends, employers, and therapists. Prior to making a telephone call to request a therapy appointment, Beth had already decided that her needs were less important than the busy schedule of the therapist and had taken the therapist's needs into consideration, and unconsciously prepared herself for one more disappointment, telling the child within that: "you really can handle this yourself." By discussing the telephone message with Beth during the first session, analyzing it with her, and with humor and sincerity assuring her that she did not have to take care of the therapist too: the feelings of fear and abandonment, shame, and low-self-esteem of the frightened child within, became, with the first telephone call, a focus in therapy. If that message is ignored, so is the child.

In the first session, Beth's forced relaxed appearance and confusion, and her apparent lack of concern for, and detachment from the pain of her abusive memories from childhood, is another attempt to protect the therapist or parental substitute figures from the insecurities, fears, and emotions of the child. By stating to Beth that, "I don't expect you to trust me so early in our relationship," the therapist is both modeling that there is a psychological boundary between two individuals, and stating to the child, "You don't have to protect me from your feelings" and "I can accept you for who you are."

As stated earlier, children in alcoholic families frequently become need satisfying objects of parents, and therefore develop bond permanence to them, and then to other parental substitutes, including partners, therapists, and frequently even their own children. Psychological boundary invasions early in life lead to exhaustion in other relationships. It is difficult to truly be available to friends and partners if an individual can't trust her/his ability to protect himself/herself from the feelings, thoughts, and needs of other individuals. As internal boundaries develop, so does the ability to establish trust in relationships.

If the Adult Child was also sexually abused in childhood, he/she will also have difficulty maintaining physical boundaries in relationships. Joe was twenty-two and had been in the process of recovery from alcoholism for three years. He sat in the chair farthest from me in the counseling office. It was his third session. He spoke quietly, staring out the window. "Will you hold me if I cry?" "No," I replied, "but I will listen and be here." He relaxed and moved his chair a bit closer. Joe had referred himself to therapy because of continual depression. He had recently stopped a one-year relationship after he had become sexually involved with his male counselor. This had been Joe's first adult relationship. His last counselor had held him when he cried. It had felt good to be held.

In reporting his own childhood history, Joe spoke warmly of his mother, "She was an alcoholic like me. My dad died when I was very young. I don't think my mother ever got over his death. She started drinking heavily when he died. She was lonely, so was I. I used to go into her room at night when I was six or seven. I was terrified at night and started sleeping with Mom every night. She hugged me and it felt good, even though I didn't like the whiskey on her breath. It frightened me, but I didn't know why. She'd hug me, kiss me, then rub my genitals. She'd ask me to caress her breasts. We were both lonely. I was scared and it felt good and bad. We made love when I was eleven. I know it was wrong, but you have to understand that my mother was a good woman. My mom died four years ago of alcoholism. I miss her. I loved her and hated her because of a secret I could never tell. We'd drink together and the pain would stop. We were both alcoholic. I feel so crazy and always have. Am I crazy?"

Adult Children like Joe have felt crazy most of their lives. It is frequently the parent who gave them the most attention and nurturing (although conditional) who also abused them sexually. Frequently, both parents were abused by their parents as children and lacked unconditional nurturing in their own families. They have come to the marriage as children, not adults, and have great difficulty meeting their own children's needs without violation of their boundaries because of their own early boundary violations.

In Joe's case, it was important that early in treatment he learn cognitively that the characteristics he developed in younger years were survival adaptions of a healthy mind, not a crazy one. Joe had little understanding when he came into counseling for the second time that his last therapist had been abusive to him and had violated his boundaries.

Individuals who have been sexually abused, either overtly or covertly, have great difficulty understanding the differences between affection, nurturing, and sexuality, this confusion often results in further abuse. They experience extremely low self-esteem, and feel desirable only when fulfilling the needs and expectations of others. Sexual abuse survivors carry with them a lifelong history of internalized shame, feeling responsible for the abuse and the pain of the entire family system. It was important for Joe that the therapist understand the extent of his ambivalence towards his mother and validate both his love for her as his nurturer, and his anger at her violation. The child locked within him needed assurance that a need for nurturing is the hallmark of normal childhood and that the abuse wasn't his fault. In Joe's case, both his physical and psychological boundaries had been violated all his life. He had attempted to construct external boundaries through his isolation.

Part of the *cognitive life raft* for sexual abuse survivors is the development of rules in relationships to protect them from further abuse while internal boundaries are developed in the process of therapy. The development of cognitive understanding of the characteristics of sexual abuse survivors and the concept of boundaries is also a protection for the survivor from violating the boundaries of others.

Myths and stigmas regarding sexual abuse continue to serve as barriers to the victims and perpetrators seeking treatment. Even though statistics indicate that one in four children in the United States have been sexually abused, myths still exist that young girls and boys reporting sexual abuse in their families are chronic liars seeking attention; that incest victims are only the underachieving, acting-out kids in school; that abuse ends at the age of eighteen; that perpetrators of sexual abuse can easily be identified as crazed men and women who attack all children with whom they have contact; and that these parents hate their children.

Sexual abuse tends to be multigenerational in families. Frequently, both parents have lifelong need for love and nurturing and have difficulty assuming the parent or spouse role in their new family. They both tend to have strong dependency needs; difficulty with boundaries, histories of alcohol or substance abuse; and difficulty with social skills which would allow them to get their dependency needs met from other adults. It is important for the therapist to understand sexual abuse dynamics in a family as a process, not merely an act, and for the entire family, whenever possible, to be engaged in the treatment process. Other children in the family, who are not the primary overt victim of the abuse (either sexual or physical) are frequently aware of the abuse and are sometims witnesses. These children, who are also victims by nature of the awareness of the abuse, are frequently untreated. Sometimes the children who witness the abuse feel not only violated, but helpless and impotent as well, and often suffer as much psychological trauma as the primary victim.

Many survivors of either sexual or physical abuse in the alcoholic family have felt that they have actually suffered more trauma from telling of the abuse, and not being believed and validated, than from the actual abuse. Many therapists unknowingly further this lack of validation to the inner child by not asking about childhood histories of abuse or by simply focusing on uncovering repressed memory as somehow *fact* of the abuse. It is our belief that the *feelings* of abuse be validated to the child whether memory is present or not. Digging for memory is often a dangerous disrespect for the needed defensive structure of the individual.

Many Adult Children have difficulty expressing feelings verbally, or have throughout their lives used intellectualization as a defense against feeling. With these individuals, the use of art or symbolic representations of history prove to be far more effective in early assessment, as well as in the process of building a relationship in therapy. "Talk Therapy" frequently is not effective with some individuals early in the process.

Working with an individual in the construction of a three generational genogram aids the therapist in gaining a broader perspective of the adult's life while presenting the child with a panographic representation of the multigenerational grief in his/her family. The representation to the child states graphically that, "The difficulties in your family that you have always assumed exclusive guilt for started long before you were born, and perhaps before the birth of your parents." An individual may remember cognitively that grandparents or great grandparents were alcoholic, but may not have emotionally integrated the information until it is symbolically presented to the child within through a visual medium. One individual responded to the panorama of history visually presented her with relief and tears, "How could I have caused the alcoholism in my family, it was there long before I was born."

Simply knowing the facts about one's history does not mean that one has unconsciously integrated the message inherent in that collection of facts. The construction of a three generational genogram also aids the therapist in the collection of important information. Anniversary dates, for instance, are frequently times when the client's internal loss file is unconsciously opened up, which leads to overwhelming depression and frequently, suicidal ideation. The fact of the loss anniversary had never been realized consciously until focused on and brought to conscious awareness by the therapist. It is no mystery, for instance, given our understanding of bond permanence and child development, that an individual may become suicidal or severely depressed during the month of

June, when June was the anniversary of a parent's death, or that an individual may experience a wish to die when reaching the age of the parent's death. The extent of family loyalty in this population is far reaching. Some Adult Children, for instance, have felt like failures all their lives because they could never complete high school. When these individuals see graphically, on a genogram, that they didn't allow themselves to achieve an educational level beyond that of a parent, they may realize that the issue is one of loyalty, not failure. It may be possible, with awareness, to release the chains of bondage and take back choice regarding education.

Suicides in families are frequently multigenerational. The memories and repressed grief regarding exact dates and times of death are often like loaded revolvers stored in an individual's unconscious. Working with individuals with extensive delayed grief, without awareness of important unconscious anniversary dates, is akin to agreeing to lead an expedition across the Pacific Ocean, equipped only with a compass and charts illustrating the waterways of the Bering Sea.

Sometimes, tools, like the use of Progressive Life Drawings in therapy (illustrated on the following pages), aid the child within in the expression of feelings and unconscious memory. Seeing the progression of drawings from age five to age sixty-five frequently assists understanding the powerful effects of repressed material in mapping future life directions.

Rose was forty-seven when she referred herself to therapy. She had been in counseling and therapy a number of times before, due to periods of depression, but had never worked on issues related to being an Adult Child. The first set of pictures, age five to forty-seven, were drawn by Rose early in the therapy relationship; pictures reflecting ages forty-seven to ninety-seven were drawn after Rose had been in therapy for a year.

Rose was raised in a family with a father who was alcoholic and a co-dependent mother. She was the youngest of seven children and remembered having very little contact with her mother, and being left alone in the care of brothers and sisters who were frequently abusive to her, as they too had little parental attention and structure. The pictures drawn by Rose of the ages between three months and three years show her tied to her crib. Some of her most painful early memories were of being pinned to her crib by her distraught mother for hours at a time. Ages three to five reflect Rose's feelings of being the scapegoat of brothers and sisters. She remembered with terror being stepped on, being buried, and being locked in a shed with bees and needing to make enough fuss and scream loud enough to get her mother's attention. By age eleven, Rose was cooking the family dinners while her mother worked. She remembered the awful dinner table scenes where no one was satisfied and Dad was drunk and making fun of her cooking. Rose remembered age sixteen as a happier year. Her brothers and sisters had left home, she had her first romance, and she decided to enter a convent when she completed high school at the age of eighteen to begin a life devoted to God.

Rose remembered both pain and joy in her early years in the convent, joy because of the isolation and prayer, and pain because of the continued worry about her mother, who she could rarely see due to the discipline of her Order. Her father died of alcoholism when she was twenty-five. Her mother remarried. Rose said that the man her mother remarried was also alcoholic and was also far more physically abusive than her father had been. Rose worried constantly about her mother and begged the Order to let her go home. Her mother died of a heart attack when Rose was twenty-eight. Rose felt responsible. She said her mother's death had been caused by abuse, and that she should have been home to care for her. Rose left the convent shortly after her mother's death and began drinking alcoholically. She worked in a hospital as a nurse during the days and *drank all night*. Rose said that things didn't seem to matter anymore. She had become involved with several men, all alcoholic; married a man who was psychologically abusive; and always kept a wall between herself and others. Rose frequently said when discussing the years that followed her mother's death, "I was walking around making the motions of living every day and drinking every night, but it was my mother that had my heart."

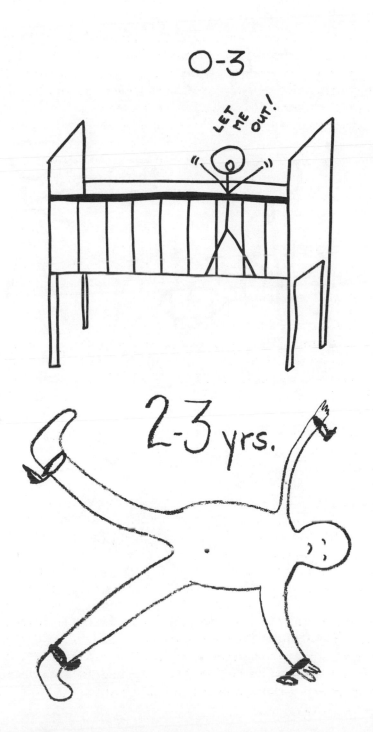

29 - 45

34-38

INTIMACY                    NEW WORK

## 67

### A NEW AGE

**SPIRITUAL UNITY**

**NEW INSIGHTS**

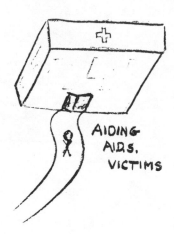

**AIDING A.I.D.S. VICTIMS**

## 77

**INTEGRATION**

### THE FOUR R'S:

REVEALING
RELATING
READING
RE-CREATING

87

COMPANIONSHIP
INTIMACY
JOY

97

IT'S TIME TO GO HOME

Rose, like many Children of Alcoholics, developed an ideal fantasy mother who was there and protected her. Her guilt for her mother's life and death protected the helpless feeling of abandonment, as well as the rage for being tied to a crib and then placed in the care of other angry and abandoned children. Rose's anger began to emerge towards the end of her first year in therapy. She felt like she was angry at everything, but mostly at people who had let her down; friends who didn't call right back after receiving a message; auto mechanics who made her wait for her car; and her therapist who wouldn't give out her home telephone number.

Rose's current and past feelings were validated in therapy, but not her expectations of immediate and unconditional love. She was helped to focus on times in her life when she felt similar. She always returned to her feelings in the crib or to the feelings of being unsafe in the care of angry and frightened brothers and sisters. It was important for the child in Rose to understand that the feelings of rage, sadness, loss, and fear were real and valid. She was helped to understand that she had lost a part of childhood to which she had a right. It was important for the child inside to cry the tears of that early trauma and to separate the childhood feelings from the feelings of current adult disappointment. It is the right of the child to expect to be the center of parental focus (unconditional love), but it is not realistic for an adult to expect to be the center focus of partners, friends, employers, therapists or other adults.

Feeling the anger and pain of today, however, with questions from the therapist, often leads to the building of a bridge to the repressed feelings of the child of yesterday. Adult love and caring is conditional love based on the mutual needs, desires, wishes, and boundaries of two people, not one. The pain of the childhood loss of that special part of life, of being the center of the world to healthy parents, is valid and that is the pain which frequently emerges when stimulated by adult disappointments.

Part of the role of the therapist, group leader, or support system is to help construct an emotional net (feelings of safety), by developing a relationship of acceptance which allows the Adult Child to build a bridge to the child within. This allows the Adult Child to touch the child within. It give the child a face through which the tears can be cried and allows the fear and pain to be felt rather than continue to be repressed or condemned. After the tears, a new bridge can be constructed to build peer networks of support and regain the choice and spontaneity imprisoned within the frightened child of the past.

Chapter Six

# The Pain That Heals Itself

Jacob Moreno, the originator of psychodrama, was fond of saying that "incomplete terminations interfere with new beginnings," i.e., we must complete our psychological business with losses of the past before we are ready to move on and form new attachments. (Moreno, 1972) Minimally, several conditions are requisite, however, before grief or "unfinished business" can be resolved. First, the individual must be able to acknowledge the reality of the loss. (Worden, 1982) However, what if we are unaware that we have sustained loss and, hence, don't know that we are "stuck" in unresolved grief, that we are in denial? Denial is a defense which is essential; it makes the unbearable easier to live with; it makes it possible to live with a predicament which cannot be solved.

Frequently, an Adult Child of an alcoholic will make an appointment with one of us for consultation and present himself in a poised, self-assured manner, as he dispassionately recounts experiencing the symptoms of acute or chronic depression. This is usually quickly followed by a disclaimer that he had a near-perfect childhood with Ward and June Cleaver as parents. I may quietly think, "I believe that you believe that to be true, but you don't get here from there, you don't have overwhelming difficulties with depression unless there was trouble in paradise." The young man's dilemma is how to reconcile a perceived near-perfect childhood and a near-perfect adulthood in which he has achieved most of his stated goals with simultaneously disquieting feelings of emptiness, dissatisfaction and despair. He has, in fact, sustained a whole train of losses of which he is unaware, and until his denial is interrupted, he will lack a context for his seemingly disconnected feelings, and he will not be able to walk through and integrate his losses until he is able to acknowledge them.

Individuals grieve not only the actual experiences which they have had, but also the developmental experiences of which they have been deprived. A major deprivation for children in alcoholic families is the loss of a sense of "family" as a growth-promoting atmosphere. Alcoholic families tend to be either enmeshed "super glue" (Reid, 1985) families, in which children feel stuck like Br'er Rabbit trying to free himself from the Tar Baby (Harris, 1960) or to be detached, "blown apart" families, made up of a congerie of isolates with little expression of interpersonal connectedness and concern. In the enmeshed families, children have a difficult time separating without feeling that their need to "take wing" is experienced by the family as betrayal and abandonment. In the detached families, children feel that no one cares enough to even notice if they drift too far away, and the child will not believe that anyone will pull him back into the family to keep from losing him. Children being reared in both of these types of families experience loss — loss of autonomy in one, and loss of important connectedness in the other.

In alcoholic family systems, the parameters of healthy family functioning are violated with adverse consequences for the children. For instance, healthy family life is predicated, as we've stated in Chapters One and Two, on parents forming an intimate pairing alliance with one another, and then out of that alliance, a parental coalition for bilateral parenting of the children. (Lidz, 1963)

When one of the members of the intimate alliance develops alcoholism, a substance, alcohol, is triangulated or pulled into an intimate relationship with the developing alcoholic, thereby pushing the other intimate partner out of the way. The other partner, whom we shall call the co-alcoholic or co-dependent, attempts to continue an intimate relationship with the alcoholic for whom *person* intimacy has been replaced by *substance* intimacy. Co-dependency or a behavioral adaptation to the increasingly distorted behavior of the alcoholic begins to develop in the co-alcoholic partner, for whom *person* intimacy is now replaced by *illness* intimacy. As the scenario continues to unfold, the co-dependent partner increasingly takes up the slack left by the alcoholics accelerating inability to function appropriately, casting the co-dependent in a new role in the family drama: the over-involved *responsibility assumer* in pursuit of a *solution* to the alcoholic's unfolding *bad* behavior. This would be all well and good were there only two people in this family. The co-dependent could continue indefinitely to prop up the sagging, under-involved alcoholic, while presenting a brave, unruffled appearance to the outside world. However, the two players in this drama have children for whom they serve as role models for intimacy, marital relationships, parenting, and sex role appropriate examples of maleness and femaleness. Years later, when queried, these children, as adults, will state that their parents served as "negative role models" for them, *i.e.*, they consciously went out of their way to do things 180 degrees differently from the models their parents provided. They report always having felt *different* and believed that everyone else received a book on how to live life, but they failed to get their copy.

It is a loss to not be able to live at least part of life on automatic pilot. Parental alcoholism during the early developmental years of these children deprives both the children and the parents of effective parental participation in their lives and activities. Over the years, the authors have worked with many recovering alcoholic parents who have mourned the lost opportunity of having missed many important developmental milestones and normal family activities with their children. What is tragic is that for these parents, grief is truly multigenerational in that they, too, often times were children of alcoholic or dysfunctional parents and simply could not provide a quality of childhood experience for their own children which they themselves had not experienced. This is one of the many ways in which alcoholism is the gift that goes on giving unto the third and fourth generation if this pattern is not interrupted. An unusually high percentage of Adult Children choose to either forego forming intimate relationships, and live isolated lives, or choose not to have children.

Many state that they fear either being inadequate or abusive like their parents, or that they are simply so ill-prepared by their own childhood experience that they can't allow themselves to take the risk. Others forego bearing children out of a clear sense of still being children themselves and not willing to be pushed aside again for someone else.

Timmen Cermack, M.D., characterizes the Adult Child syndrome as an example of post-traumatic stress syndrome or delayed grief. He speaks of the process of personal empowerment as individuals reared in alcoholic families become able to acknowledge the reality of how it really was, rather than the illusion of how they wished it could have been. (Cermack, 1984) This is the first step in grief resolution: naming the loss and acknowledging its reality, rather than continuing to deny it. However, to name a thing is not to heal it, and therein lies one of the dilemmas of the current Children of Alcoholics Movement. It takes both time and external support to intergrate a loss, and the naming of the loss is only one step in the healing process. Individuals who have experienced loss strive to achieve both cognitive and emotional mastery of the experience, and many Adult Children risk feeling despair when, after reading self-help books and attending Children of Alcoholics conferences, they still feel pain. They need to be assured that they are not Humpty Dumpties whom all the King's Horses, and all the King's Men cannot put together again.

Books and conferences are attempts at mastery, and part of the grief work process, but it needs to be recognized that the process of working through childhood loss is a time-dependent, socially facilitated process which can't be hurried.

In one of the prior chapters, grief was described as the pain that heals itself, provided we do not get in our own way and provided others do not impede our working it through. It is a normal emotional state which entails making real a loss and progressively loosening out internal attachment to that which has been lost. This process is called grief work and not only encompasses the following ". . . four tasks of mourning: Task I: To accept the reality of the loss; Task II: To experience the pain of grief; Task III: To adjust to an environment in which 'that which had been lost' . . . is missing; and Task IV: To withdraw emotional energy and reinvest it in another relationship (Worden, 1982, pp. 11-15) but also encompasses a series of universal emotional reactions. A model for grief work always begins with *loss*, since real or threatened loss disrupts important attachment bonds, and sets grief work in motion. The next expected response to loss is *shock*, a state of numbness and disbelief while we collect ourselves to face this new reality. This is then followed by the stage of *denial*. It simply hasn't happened; our minds refuse to countenance the loss. *Depression* is the next anticipated emotional response to loss and is characterized by a state of sadness and a disrupted sense of well-being as we recognize our world has a hole in it. Next we tend to respond with the *if only's* which characterize the *guilt stage in grief resolution*.

In normal grief resolution, this is a transient state, during which we scan our memories to examine if we were somehow derelict, or did we somehow fail to do something which could have prevented this loss from happening. *Anger* appears next on the scene as a normal emotional response to loss and often alternates back and forth with feelings of guilt. The anger phase of grief resolution is the phase which Bowlby speaks of as "protest," and is an attempt on the part of the person to retrieve that which has been lost. Frequently we are angry with ourselves for not having prevented the loss, or for being ineffectual. Or possibly, we displace our angry feelings on to third parties and look for who is to blame, *e.g.*, our grandparents, the culture.

For children from alcoholic families, it is a sign of beginning recovery when they become able to interrupt their self-rebuke and to re-direct their anger away from themselves to someone else, eventually recognizing that no one is to blame. Anger, of course, is also harbored as a consequence of something or someone that has been lost. For example, "Why didn't you take better care of yourself?" or "How can you die? Now I'll *never* get what I need from you. I've lost my chance forever," or "It isn't fair." Lastly, if the individual is able to experience the pain associated with each step of this emotional process, and not get stuck or act out his feelings rather than feeling them, he will move on to the final stage of *reconstruction* or what Worden calls "emotional reinvestment." Although this description sounds like a cookbook for grief resolution, it is in fact a fairly complicated, long-term repetitive process wherein life presents us with opportunities again and again to complete another piece of our emotional "unfinished business." (Bellwood, 1975, p. 8)

The second step in grief resolution is to experience the feelings associated with the loss. The authors have drawn on the insights of Bruno Bettelheim (Bettelheim, 1980, pp. 19-37) and the current post-traumatic stress syndrome literature for a discussion of the impediments to this step in the grief resolution process. (Van Der Kolk, 1984) It is generally agreed that the burden of any trauma is three-fold: (1) The original trauma itself; (2) its effect on either personality development or personality integrations; and (3) the necessity of walking back through the trauma and re-experiencing it in order to integrate, *i.e.*, cognitively and emotionally master it. The keystone to the survival adaptation, which children in alcoholic families develop in order to emotionally protect themselves from their difficult life circumstances, are the defenses of denial and repression. These defenses do not alter the child's external life circumstances, but their use allows him to sustain life in the face of circumstances which seem, or in fact are, intolerable. Faced with a surplus of feeling that is evoked by a situation over which they have no control, these children respond with a surplus of denial, which has come to be characterized in the psychiatric literature as "psychic numbing," "Psychic closing off," or "affective anesthesia." (Krystal, 1984, p. 16) It is important at this point for the authors to caution the reader to bear in mind that emotional traumatization falls in the continuum from the most severe effects to the least severe effects, and to not impute the most severe effects to all individuals affected by parental alcoholism. This information is to be used judiciously and selectively.

"Affective anesthesia" and "affect intolerance" are defenses seen in individuals who have been emotionally overwhelmed, either by an acute trauma, or by cumulative chronic trauma, which is greater than the ego's capacity to integrate and greater than the degree of external support available to assist with its integration. (Krystal, 1984, p. 16) One or both of the requisite conditions which would facilitate integrating the experience may be missing: (1) The person's having the ability to feel the feelings associated with the loss, and (2) the presence of at least one other person with whom the experience can be shared, who will receive the emotional outpouring in a supportive, non-judgmental way.

In previous chapters we have discussed the extreme isolation of alcoholic families, both within the family; from other family members, as well as from sources of support in the larger community. The denial of, "There's nothing wrong here. Don't talk about it" combined with the lack of people supports for working out troubled feelings, accounts for the "affective anesthesia" we see in the members of these families. Both the co-dependent spouse and the children bear the emotional brunt of the chaotic home environment with only the aid of emotional anesthesia. The alcoholic, on the other hand, does not share their reality, his awareness is blunted by denial, blackouts and actual central nervous system anesthesia.

We are of the opinion that Adult Children from alcoholic families will not allow themselves to interrupt their denial and experience a catharsis of their feelings until there are sufficient people supports available for them in their environment. In therapy, these patients are often characterized as resistant when, in fact, they are following their internal intuitive dictates about the kind and quality of support required in order for them to be safe enough to *feel* some of their repressed hurts. Many Adult Children therapists shop for long periods of time, driven by their pain to seek help, but afraid to trust that they will not be let down. They test the water to see if it's safe enough to get in, and then, once in, test the water again and again to see if their therapist will be able to stay the course.

Many Adult Children do not view *emotion* positively, having been so overwhelmed by their emotional responses to the chaos, violence, or tension in their home lives when they were small children. The most severely traumatized have developed "affect intolerance" and are willing to go to any lengths to avoid feeling. (Krystal, 1984, p. 16) For some of these individuals, alcohol becomes their anesthetic in adulthood, just as it was for their alcoholic parents. For others, an emotionally constricted life, designed to avoid upsetting circumstances, helps them to keep their feelings in an emotional deep freeze.

". . . People who have been exposed to catastrophic events react to them with the establishment of a new style of adaptation, which centers around a restriction of affective involvement with their environment. Thus, while their autonomic nervous system continues to react to some physical and emotional stimuli, as if there were a continuous threat of annihilation, they appear to compensate for this hyperreactivity with emotional withdrawal." (Van Der Kolk/Ducey, 1984, p. 30)

Adult Children, regardless of how they have learned to temporize with their feelings, share a commonality with many other people confronted with the depth and intensity of feelings associated with grief: They become terrified that they will be blown apart or driven crazy by the intensity of what they are experiencing. Adult Children report symptoms which are quite like those reported by victims of post-traumatic stress syndrome as they begin their recovery process, *i.e.*, intermittent, partial breakdown of denial, and with it an affective "thawing"; intrusive, recurrent memories or "flashbacks" of repressed childhood experiences; disturbing nightmares; emotional hyperreactivity or startle reactions; and a wish to avoid anything that could lead to an emotional re-experiencing of the trauma.

This is the point at which the delayed grief reaction can begin to be worked through, for the Adult Child is finally able to *feel* the feelings associated with the losses. Affectivity returns with the breakthrough of traumatic memories. (Van Der Kolk/Ducey, 1984, p. 40) It is only during this period of "emotional under control" that the memories and feelings of the trauma are accessible enough to be worked through, and yet this can be a terrifying time for the person beginning a recovery period. (Van Der Kolk/Ducey, 1984, p. 40) He may characterize this phase as "falling apart" or "losing control" and may prematurely abort treatment, seeing therapy as *making him worse*. Therapists function as attachment figures or *people supports* at this point in grief resolution, helping the Adult Child to incrementally develop *affect tolerance* or psychological *muscles* as the individual slowly allows repressed memories to surface in a dosed manner. There is no coercion in this process. The therapist respects the Adult Child's defenses, recognizing the extent to which the client at times feels like a terrified animal wanting to bolt off to a place that feels emotionally safer. His pace is respected; no simple prescription is applied to how he *ought to be* working through his grief and trauma. The therapist waits patiently for the story to unfold and with the story, the once buried affects. There is no therapeutic *big bang* that leads to instantaneous resolution at this point in the process. The Adult Child can only develop new psychological *muscles* and a new vocabulary and understanding for his feelings and the meaning of his submerged life experience which is surfacing into conscious awareness ever so gradually.

In the next phase of grief resolution, if the individual has been able to stay the course, he will adjust to the reality of his environment, that is that which has been lost is missing and will never be present again, *i.e.*, he will be acknowledging the irretrievability of that which has been lost. (Worden, 1982, p. 14) Many categories of experience can constitute a loss to which one must adjust, such as: ". . . (1) material loss — of any object of value; (2) physical loss, involving part of one's body, or developmental losses suffered as one passes through the stages of life; (3) psychological loss of self-esteem, self-respect, self-confidence or the like; and (4) loss of a significant figure in one's life, either through death or through separation." (Bellwood, 1975, p. 8) Hopefully, the Adult Child at this point in the grieving process has been able to acknowledge the reality of that which has been lost, feel the feelings associated with the loss in manageable doses, and with adequate people supports, he now becomes willing to relinquish the many emotional maneuvers he has been employing to "say it isn't so." *Never* is a difficult reality for any of us to countenance, and hence, we bargain, cajole, manipulate and deny in the hope that that which has been lost can be reclaimed if we are only good enough, or clever enough to find the magical combination. In this particular phase of grief resolution, the person is finally able to admit to himself that there is no magic and that the loss is permanent and irretrievable. That is to say, he can allow himself to *know*, for instance, that he will never experience the idealized family which he so desparately wished for in childhood. He will never be a warm, secure, loved little four-year-old boy with a happy, healthy mommy and daddy, but instead, he will understand that the only repair of the past is in the present and entails allowing himself to have experiences *now* which he missed *then*, but he does this with the awareness that no amount of reparative experience will completely erase how it was "then."

A motto on a popular poster sums up this experience, "*The truth will set you free, but first it will make you miserable.*" In effect, the person becomes willing to relinquish his sense of entitlement to reparations for wrongs done in childhood. He realizes that although it was unfair that he missed some essential experiences in childhood, the rest of the world does not owe him a debt. It was unfair that things happened as they did, but he finally becomes willing to let go of attempting to extract his emotional needs from others via emotional blackmail.

This step frees him for the final task of grief resolution: to be willing to withdraw his emotional investment in that which has been lost and move on to form a new attachment. For Adult Children, this step often comes after they have been able to see their parents and their family from a multigenerational perspective. It is difficult to hang on to blame, anger, and disappointment when the person sees that his parents were themselves burdened with the unresolved grief of their own multigenerational transmission process. In looking back three generations, familiar patterns emerge which help to explain the life circumstances that his parents and grandparents wrestled with.

In a sense, an Adult Child from an alcoholic family then becomes like a shopper who goes to the supermarket to buy artichokes, only to find that there are none on the shelves. He walks up and down the aisles looking for what he needs with no success, and finally asks the checker where they are kept. The checker says, "We don't have any. We don't carry artichokes here." Some Adult Children, unable to let go of their attachment to the past, continue to wander up and down the aisles or repeatedly bang on the checkout-counter, demanding their artichokes. Others finally understand and, rather than denying their need and saying they don't like artichokes or that they don't need them, simply shop at another supermarket. Full recovery entails recognizing that many of our parents didn't stock their shelves with what we needed because they in turn never received essential supplies from their families. Rather than continuing to bang on the checkout-counter of life, or rail at their parents to give them something their parents never got, and hence, cannot give, these recovering Adult Children begin to recognize that only they can create for themselves the reparative life experiences which make some restitution for the past. They become their own "good parents," providing themselves with the self-soothing, self-care and self-respect for which they have longed, not in the defensively self-reliant way of the past, but instead with a sense of empowerment in knowing that they have a choice at this point in their lives and it is their responsibility now to create the optimal life circumstances for the child within them. They become willing to move on and attach to life, feeling sadness, not despair, about the past.

# Chapter Seven

# I'd Always Dreamed of
# Riding a Merry-Go-Round Horse

## Behavior Change in Adult Children

Janet was on her way to the grocery store with her four adolescent boys. It was a beautiful summer day. When they reached the entrance to the store, Janet saw a line of children waiting to ride the brightly colored merry-go-round horse. Her thoughts went back to other summer days in childhood. She remembered watching other children jump on similar horses and wait while their parents dug in their pockets for dimes. She remembered the children giggling with delight when the coins were put in the slots and the horses jerked and moved up and down. Janet's eyes filled with tears as she remembered that her alcoholic parents were rarely there on such summer days. If they were, they were usually in such a hurry to get home to their beer or whiskey that they could never take the time to let her ride. She remembered one day when she was four begging her dad for just one dime. She was slapped and she never asked again. As Janet stood watching,

almost in a daze, she wondered if the grief would ever stop.
Then it occurred to her that she was now an adult and could
possibly. . . "Why not?" she said out loud. Janet reached into
her pocket and found a quarter, then got in line with the other
children. Her four sons stopped and looked at her in amazement. The oldest screeched, "Mom, you're not going to, are
you?" "Why not?" she replied, almost talking to herself again.
Her boys all laughed. Two of them turned bright shades of
pink and said they'd wait for her in the store, although they
watched from just inside the store with delight. The remaining
two stood watching their mother with amazement and laughed
with her. The boys remembered times in the past when they
thought their mother was a bit too serious and too hard-work-
ing, and how they were delighted with these times when they
would all spontaneously play, laugh, and tease each other.
One of the boys saw a friend and yelled, "Would you believe
my mother is riding a merry-go-round horse?" The boy came
to join them. He spent lots of time at their house and was not
surprised, "Yeah, that's just like your mom," he said, laughing. "Your mom is really something else. She's a real kick."

Janet, like many Adult Children, had not always been "a
real kick." In earlier times, prior to working through her own
delayed grief process, she had been extremely serious, constantly in control, perfectionistic, frequently depressed, sixty
pounds overweight, and suffered from constant physical
problems like ulcers, headaches, and back problems. Janet
was also so worried about raising her children in the beginning
that she had little energy left to enjoy them. She, like many
Children of Alcoholics, "didn't know what normal was." She
constantly read books on child rearing and took numerous
classes on parenting, but felt constantly as though she were a
bad parent.

"Alcoholism is the Gift that Goes on Giving." Oftentimes
Adult Children who have not cried their own childhood tears
find the same patterns in their own family systems, with or
without the alcohol, that they feared and hated as children.
They often feel distant from their own kids and see the same
chaos developing in their new family systems as existed in their

old. Some, rather than distancing, become so enmeshed with their children that they have difficulty setting limits, and following through, and can't tell the difference between their child's pain and their own. They have difficulty tolerating normal emotions in their children, and sometimes see unresolved conflict and grief functioning as another "elephant in the living room," in much the same way alcohol had in their early childhood family. They lack spontaneity and choice and frequently lose the joy of experiencing their own children's development just as they did their own childhood years. One ten-year-old boy told me of his experience with his parents who were both Adult Children, "It is no fun going on trips with my mom and dad. They once saved up to take us on a trip to the Grand Canyon. We were so excited until we realized that the goal of the trip was getting there and then the goal was to come home. It was a drag."

Parenting, weight loss, or the joys of experiencing one's life rather than tedious survival cannot be found in self-help books or through attending behavior modification classes. The authors believe that the effects of early childhood trauma cannot be reduced by adding more information about perfection to an already over laden image ideal. Adult Children have experienced enough significant trauma in childhood to encase the most important parts of themselves in ice, and with that freezing have lost their ability to make choices. The level of spontaneity encased within that child of the past cannot be unthawed by merely learning new steps to the dance.

Bob and Ann referred themselves for marital therapy after reading an article on Adult Children. Prior to coming into therapy they had read countless books on fair fighting, marital communication, and child rearing, as well as having attended countless seminars on these subjects. They had been excited by each one and had believed they *had found the answer* to a happier marriage. They had studied hard and practiced each new technique and after a time fought even more about the other's seeming unwillingness to follow the methods learned. Bob and Ann had read the characteristics of Adult Children of alcoholics and had originally made an appointment with the hope of *finding one more answer*. There was a lot of humor in the first session as it was pointed out countless times that they each appeared to be entering therapy with the same degree of perfectionism that they had about other things in their life, like marriage and child rearing. They were told, "There are no 'A's' in here. You sound like you wanted to come here to get rid of the characteristics of being Adult Children in two and a half weeks. Do either of you ever let up on yourselves?" They presented examples of their disagreements and talked about techniques they had used to solve the problems to no avail. One example they gave dealt with the budget. First, he had tried to handle all the finances and had methodically drawn up a budget that had not made provisions for entertainment costs. Ann had objected and Bob felt injured saying, "You do it, then." Then Ann tried it. She blamed Bob for overspending, which had resulted in their getting into debt. Bob had said that Ann hadn't made allowances for the money he needed for lunches and she responded, "You never asked me for that money or let me know what you needed." Bob said, "You should have known."

Throughout their counseling, it was apparent that most of their difficulty stemmed from injured feelings that were out of proportion to reality events. Ann felt constantly attacked by Bob and felt that he never approved of her or respected what she did. Bob felt that Ann never responded to his needs, although it was clear that he never stated them. Both attempted to read each other's minds and carefully processed responses to questions and needs without ever stating them, then accused the other of lack of sensitivity. Therapy sessions were full of statements like, "But you never asked," or "I never said that." Most of their communication was heard by injured children and most of their accusations to each other were the words never said to abusive, critical, or abandoning parents. The bond permanence to the once-demanding parent had been substituted with bond permanence to a new spouse.

The authors agree with the work of both Berkowitz (1985) and the Blancks (1968) who base their framework on the work of Margaret Mahler who observed that couples who

come from homes where unconditional love and healthy
mirroring are not provided by parents tend to seek unmet
needs from others in their lives, including partners. These
individuals attempt to continue to prove their own perfection
of an idealized image by seeking constant affirmation from
other adults or by demands from others for total and unconditional acceptance. As Mahler states, "such symbiotic union
longing for merger is also expressed in the wish to be completely understood by the partner without having to articulate
one's thoughts or wishes verbally." (Berkowitz, 1985, p. 233)

Because each in the partnership sees the other as a powerful
person on whom they are dependent for survival, actions and
words are met with great anxiety and interpreted by each other
as threats of abandonment. As stated by Berkowitz: "Protective defenses in the spouse against anxiety about rejection are
persistently misconstrued as the spouse's indifference. Each
partner is afraid to reach out to the other for what is needed.
The dread of disappointment is an iron-clad conviction as a
result of early painful experiences." (Berkowitz, 1985, p. 235)

The role of the therapist with the couple or family is similar
to working with an individual: to build a bridge to the child
within, to aid the child in expressing and crying the tears, and
to allow the child once held hostage the freedom as an adult to
take back choice in her/his life. Without the interpretation of
the historical communication that is foremost in the interaction and without the help of each individual to walk back
through the trauma and gain mastery over the pain of the past,
each decision faced or plan attempted by the couple or family
will be dictated by the pain of the past rather than by the
creativity and needs of the present family or relationship.
Even an issue as simple as developing a family budget will be
complicated by a family reunion each time the couple
attempts to communicate about the issue.

Behavior change in Adult Children is the end result of the
grief work process, not a master plan designed and memorized
in order to attain a more perfect self. Our caseloads are full of
individuals who have gone through program after program
designed for sexual addiction without success, or have

become celibate and become extremely depressed; or they have switched a sexual addiction to another compulsive behavior and then attacked themselves for their failures, which only further supports more compulsive behavior. Frequently, individuals who have originally come into therapy to "cure" an addiction and have focused instead on walking through early childhood trauma, have found that their addictive behavior decreases after the grief work without their even noticing it. They find themselves more capable of assertiveness in relationships and in their professions without consciously practicing elaborate skills. "Yeses" or "no's" come from a place of internal comfort with choice rather than from some master plan in the self-help literature.

Working through the process of grief allows the self, once held hostage, the freedom to live life, rather than being held captive by the unmet needs and expectations of others. It allows the individual the spontaneity and choice of living in the present, rather than in the past or future.

Children raised in alcoholic families who have not worked through their own delayed grief suffer from the agonizing impairment of being emotionally color-blind and are allowed only tunnel vision when faced with day-to-day choices. Individuals with such an emotional visual impairment literally do not know that they function in life with a disability until offered the opportunity to see through corrective lenses. Making a choice to enter the process of walking back through the trauma is literally choosing to regain emotional vision, rather than retaining the impaired vision of past generations. Frequently, the grief process involves experiencing the grief of several generations as well as the losses of one's own childhood. In Joan's case, for example, it entailed not only experiencing the pain of her early childhood memories of spending hours practicing dance while other children played outside, but also entailed experiencing the pain of her mother's unmet fantasies and dreams. Taking back one's life from the chains of bond permanence to one's parent involves feeling the pain of being held captive while other children played, feeling the terror of the realization of felt abandonment, as well as feeling the parent's fears, rage, and pain which the child had absorbed. Joan cried tears for her mother's life before she was able to cry tears for the child within herself held captive by her mother's pain. It was, in fact, her mother who had grieved her entire life the loss of dance, not Joan. As Joan retrieved each memory from the past, she was able to separate her mother's pain from the pain experienced by her child of the past. As each painful memory returned, she regained more and more of her own unmet dreams, life experiences, emotions, and fantasies. In one session she was able to experience the rage of the years lost in trying to attain her mother's dream: "I can't believe I almost killed myself because I couldn't dance when I really didn't want to be a dancer in the first place. I almost killed myself for my mother's pain."

After the tears, Joan regained choice in her own life. She allowed herself new experiences which led to an expansion of her own choices. She realized that she had never made the choice not to marry, or not to have children, and that the choices that she had once believed to be her own had, in reality, been the desires and unmet needs of past generations. She grieved the loss of childhood play and of toys she never had, and most of all, the pain of never having had unconditional love. With the process of emotional separation from her mother came a new awareness that it never was applause that she had wanted, but instead, to be loved and nurtured, and that applause from others would never fill the emptiness of a lost childhood. As she put it, "I have lived my life trying to give my mother a life so that finally she would love me. Now, at the age of thirty-two I am grieving the loss of myself and just beginning to see my own life before me. There are so many choices, but at least now I know that I am alive. Now that I have myself, I feel this strange sadness at never having had a mother. It's as if she died, and I'm mourning her death."

After the process of grief comes a new process of mourning. It is not possible to mourn the real losses of others until an individual has become a separate self. Grief is the process of taking back one's life, and mourning is the process of feeling the sadness of the loss of others. For some, it is the real loss of parents as well as brothers and sisters. For others, it is the loss of the fantasy family that will never be. When an Adult Child has given a face to his own child held hostage within, and freed that child from emotional bondage to the parent, he can begin to give real faces to those around him. He begins to see his alcoholic parents as real men or women with pain and history, rather than as projected demons or "perfect" people on pedestals. He begins to mourn the loss of relationship with brothers and sisters and to recognize the experiences that his siblings also had in the family without feeling responsible or guilty for their pain or loss. When others in the family can be seen as separate individuals, it is possible to develop new relationships with them, taking into account who they really are, not who they are expected or wished to be.

It is both freeing and sad to realize that an alcoholic parent or sibling may never recover from alcoholism, or that a co-dependent parent may never achieve the freedom of living her/his life rather than simply existing. In seeing significant others in our lives as real people with real faces, we are also able to see that the decisions which they have made in their lives are their choices rather than our responsibilities. Sometimes their choices involve further losses in our lives: losses of shared experience, losses of shared holidays or quality time for our children with grandparents, aunts, or uncles. With each loss there is not only more mourning, but also the freedom of choice.

Perhaps it may mean seeing a parent only when he/she is sober, and, therefore, seeing less of her/him than would be possible were he/she to choose to enter recovery. Perhaps it will mean fewer conversations on the telephone if we make a decision to limit the drinking or abusive behavior which interferes with communication. Seeing an emotional world of color, rather than the sterile fantasy projections of black and white, means regaining the ability to spontaneously experience the joyful and nurturing moments in life as well as the times of sadness, anger, and tears. Some Adult Children early in the grief process ask, "Will there be a time when all this sadness and disappointment will be over?" The answer is, "No, I hope you will always be able to experience the full range of emotions." The span of colorful feelings between the starkness of black and white does not mean a life without pain and sorrow. It means the ability to feel the full range of human emotion in the present.

After the tears, Children of Alcoholics begin to experience new balance in their lives. Often this means new experiences of play, alone time, quality time with children, and new feelings of spirituality. It frequently means the ending of old relationships and the beginning of new ones.

Children of Alcoholics frequently live their lives with caseloads rather than friendships, and often, after having resolved their grief, they begin to set limits which result in angry responses by members of their caseload who cannot adapt to a relationship of equality due to their own dependency needs. Sometimes, as in Joan's case, it may mean the changing of career choices based on one's own needs rather than on generational legacies. The graphs on the following page reflect the changes in the balance of Joan's life after the grief work. The first graph represents the time preoccupied by early life experiences before her injury, and the second represents her life after her grief work was completed in therapy.

After the tears, Adult Children take back spontaneity into their own lives. They free the child within from the bondage of past generations and with that freedom regain choice. As illustrated in the story of Janet at the beginning of the chapter, there is the realization that losses in the past can never be completely regained in the present. Janet was not able to ride a merry-go-round horse at the age of five years, nor was she able to experience many of the joys normal for a five-year-old. She realized, however, that although age five was gone forever, she could reclaim certain experiences in adult life. Riding a merry-go-round horse at age thirty-five was not the same as it would have been at age five, but *part* of the experience could be reclaimed through her new-found freedom and spontaneity. It is not possible to retrieve the lost experiences of childhood: we can never be eight-years-old again, but we can develop as

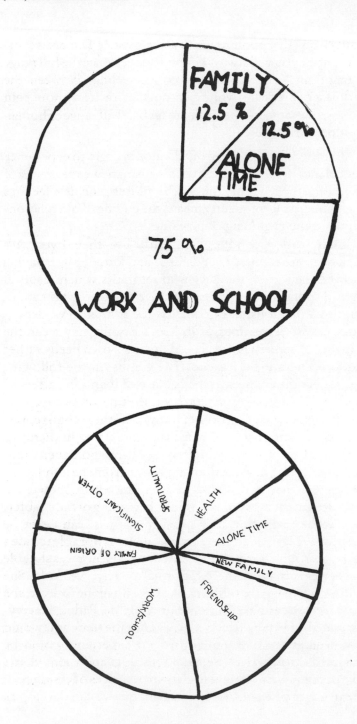

adults a range of experience that was never possible as children.

We can never again be loved unconditionally, as was our right as infants and small children, but we can ask for nurturing needs as adults.

We can begin new rituals for this and future generations even though we can never regain the holidays lost in childhood. After the tears, we can open up to a life of touch and warmth that was not possible when the child inside us was still encased in ice.

Ann had attended a workshop for Adult Children of alcoholics. She had increasingly experienced pain throughout the day as she realized that she would never be eight-years-old again. Instead of forcing herself to go to work the next day, she decided to allow herself the time and space to experience her sadness. When she got home, she called her best friend who was also an Adult Child. She sobbed over the telephone and told her friend, "I realized today that I will never be eight-years-old again." She asked her friend if she would come over. The friend appeared at the door of Ann's house with popcorn, coloring books, crayons, peanut butter and jelly sandwiches, and "jammies with feet." Her friend didn't tell Ann that she shouldn't feel what she felt, but instead told her to put on the "jammies with feet," and then held her friend for hours while she sobbed, grieving the loss of an important time in childhood. Then Ann and her friend drank cocoa, ate popcorn and peanut butter and jelly sandwiches, and laid on their stomachs on the floor coloring in the coloring books for the rest of the evening.

With her friend's support, Ann realized that she would never be eight-years-old again, but could experience the reparative joy of being a *forty-five-year-old* eight-year-old, and feel the warmth and nurturing of a caring "cookie person" friend. She could never reclaim experiences lost to her in childhood, but could open her life up to new experiences of play, joy, and nurturing, after the tears.

## Generation's Birth

For thrity years I was locked inside
The birth canal of a youthful bride;
A mother whose spirit kept me there
Frozen from her love and care.
Her own head locked in rigid bones,
A martyr that her mother owned.
To hear her heart beat drove me wild
I knew I was my mother's child.


I was covered from start with perspiration,
Trapped, but fighting to be free.
Mother floated in whisky's sleep;
The pills that calmed her, frightened me.
Grandmother sat no strength to share
Cross-legged, rigid in her chair
Reading words of procreation
While mother hid from God's damnation.
To hear her heart beat made me wild
I knew I was my mother's child.


I fought the liquid life that fed me
Fought the molecules of time
Battled the generations that bred me
Fought for strength and assertive mind
Married man, but kept my distance
Had his child, but held resistance.
To hear her heart beat kept me wild
I knew I was my mother's child.

*My own child had her life before me*
*I won the battle to let her go*
*I worked my job and let her know me*
*I built my life and watched hers grow.*
*I won the battle of independence;*
*Freedom from generation's womb*
*But not the struggle against resistance*
*Locked outside of peaceful room.*
*To hear my heart beat drove her wild*
*She knew she was her daughter's child.*

*by Jane Middelton (Moz)*
*from Juggler In a Mirror (1980)*

# Bibliography

Alther, Lisa. 1984. *Other Women*. New York: A Signet book.

American Psychiatric Association. 1980. *Diagnostic and Statistical Manual of Mental Disorders*, 3rd edition. Washington, D.C.: American Psychiatric Association.

Arieti, Silvano, and Bemporad, Jules. 1978. *Severe and Mild Depression: The Psychotherapeutic Approach*. New York: Basic Books, Inc.

Beck, Aaron T.; Rush, John A.; Shaw, Brian F.; and Emery, Gary. 1979. *Cognitive Therapy of Depression*. New York: The Guilford Press.

Bellwood, Lester R., Ph.D. Spring, 1975. "Grief work in Alcoholism Treatment." *Alcohol, Health and Research World*.

Bergmann, Martin S., and Jucovy, Milton E. (Eds). 1982 *Generations of the Holocaust*. New York: Basic Books, Inc.

Berkowitz, David. Summer 1985. "Self Object Needs and Marital Dysharmony." *The Psychoanalytic Review*. Vol. 72, No. 2, pp. 229-237.

Bettelheim, Bruno. 1980. "Trauma and Re-integration." *Surviving and Other Essays*. New York: Vintage Books.

Black, Claudia. 1982. *It Will Never Happen To Me*. Denver: M.A.C. Printing, Publication Division.

Blanck, R., and Blanck, G. 1968. *Marriage and Personal Development*. New York: Columbia University Press.

Bowlby, John. 1980 *Attachment and Loss: Volume III, Loss, Sadness and Depression*. New York: Basic Books, Inc.

Brown, Stephanie, Ph.D. 1983. "A Developmental Framework for Understanding the Adult Children of Alcoholics." Children of Alcoholics Conference. Los Angeles, CA. October 8-10.

Burgan, Jean, A.C.S.W. 1974. Tacoma, Washington.

Burns, David. 1980. *Feeling Good: The New Mood Therapy*. New York: A Signet book.

Calogeres, Roy. Spring 1985. "Early Object Relations Conflict in Marital Disharmony." *Psychoanalytic Review*. Vol. 72, No. 1, pp. 31-53.

Carnes, Patrick. 1983. *The Sexual Addiction.* New York: CompCare Publications.

Cermak, Timmen, M.D. 1984. "Children of Alcoholics: The Power of Reality and the Reality of Power." *Children of Alcoholics Conference.* Seattle, WA. June 8-10.

Cork, R. Margaret. 1969. *The Forgotten Children.* Toronto: Paper Jacks.

Dwinell, Lorie. May-June 1985. "Walking Through Grief: The Essential Elements." *Focus on Family.* pp. 18-19.

Dwinell, Lorie. January-February 1986. "Working Through Grief: The Pain That Heals Itself." *Focus on Family.* pp. 24-28.

Elkind, David. 1981. *The Hurried Child: Growing Up Too Fast Too Soon.* Reading, Mass.: Addison-Wesley Publishing Co.

Flach, Frederic F., and Draghi, Suzanne C. 1975. "An Eclectic Approach to Depression." in Flach, Frederic F., and Draghi, Suzanne C., Eds. *The Nature and Treatment of Depression.* New York: John Wiley & Sons

Flach, Frederic F. 1974. *The Secret Strength of Depression.* Philadelphia: Lippincott.

Fraiberg, Selma H. 1959. *The Mask Years.* New York: Charles Scribner's Sons.

Freud, Anna. (1936) *The Ego and the Mechanisms of Defense.* New York: International Universities Press, 2nd ed., 1966.

Freud, Anna. (1965) *Normality and Pathology in Childhood Assessment Development.* New York: International Universities Press.

Freud, Sigmund. (1920) *Beyond the Pleasure Principle.* London: Hogarth Press, 1955.

Freud, Sigmund. (1925) "Inhibitions, Symptoms and Anxiety." *Standard Edition,* 20:167. London: Hogarth Press, 1959.

Freyberg, Joan T. Spring 1984. "The Psychoanalytic Treatment of Narcissim." *Psychoanalytic Psychology.* Vol. 1, No. 2, pp. 99-112.

Furst, Sidney F. (Ed) 1967. *Psychic Trauma.* New York: Basic Books, Inc.

Greenleaf, Jael. 1984. "The Alcoholic Family as a Learning System." *Children of Alcoholics Conference.* Seattle, WA. June 8-10.

Greif, Ann. Fall 1985. "Masochism in the Therapist." *The Psycho-analytic Review.* Vol. 72, No. 3, pp. 491-501.

Harris, Joel Chandler. 1960. *Uncle Remus Stories As Told by Jane Shaw.* Glasgow, Scotland: Collins.

Herzog, James. 1982. "World Beyond Metaphor: Thoughts on the Transmission of Trauma." in Bergmann & Jucovy. *Generations of the Holocaust.* New York: Basic Books, Inc.

Kissen, Morton. 1985. "The Therapeutic Use of Self and Object Presentations in the Treatment of Character Disorders." *Psycho-analytic Practice.* Adelphi Society for Psychoanalysis and Psycho-therapy, Inc. Monograph. pp. 25-46.

Kline, Nathan. 1974. *From Sad to Glad.* New York: Ballantine Books.

Kohut, H. 1971. *The Analysis of Self.* New York: International Universities Press.

Krystal, Henry, M.D. 1984. "Psychoanalytic Views on Human Emotional Damages." in Van Der Kolk, Bessel A., Eds. *Post-Traumatic Stress Disorder: Psychological and Biological Sequelae.* Washington, D.C.: American Psychiatric Press, Inc.

Lawson, Gary; Peterson, James F.; and Lawson, Ann. 1983 *Alcohol-ism and the Family: A Guide to Treatment and Prevention.* Rockville, Maryland: Aspen Publications.

Lewinsohn, Peter M.; Munoz, Ricardo S.; Youngren, Mary Ann; and Zeiss, Antonette M. 1978. *Control Your Depression.* Englewood Cliffs: Prentice-Hall.

Lidz, Theodore. 1963. *The Family and Human Adaptation.* New York: International Universities Press.

Lowen, Alexander. 1983. *Narcissism.* New York: Collier Books.

Mahler, Margaret S. 1968. *On Human Symbiosis and Vicissitudes of Individuation.* New York: International Universities Press.

Mahler, Margaret S., et. al. 1975. *The Psychological Birth of the Human Infant.* New York: Basic Books, Inc.

Malmquist, Carl P. 1975. "Depression in Childhood." in Flach, Frederic S., and Draghi, Suzanne C., Eds. *The Nature and Treat-ment of Depression.* New York: John Wiley and Sons.

Middelton, Jane, and Harris, Susan. 1980. *Juggler in a Mirror.* Kirkland, Washington: Arthur-Ward Publications.

Middelton, Jane. September-October 1984. "Double Stigma: Sexual Abuse Within the Alcoholic Family." *Focus on Family*. pp. 6-11.

Middelton, Jane. January-February 1985. "Adult Children of Alcoholics Become Parents: A 'Pioneering' Effort." *Focus on Family*. pp. 37-38.

Miller, Alice. 1981. *The Drama of the Gifted Child*. New York: Basic Books, Inc.

Miller, Alice. 1984. *For Your Own Good*. New York: Farrar, Straus, Giroux.

Mitscherlich, Alexander and Margarete. 1975. *The Inability to Mourn*. New York: The Grove Press, Inc.

Montgomery, Jill. Fall 1985. "The Return of Masochistic Behavior in the Therapist." *The Psychoanalytic Review*. Vol. 72, No. 3, pp. 503-511.

Moreno, Jacob. 1972. *Psychodrama*. Beacon, New York: Beacon House, Inc.

Paykel, Eugene S. 1975. "Environmental Variables in the Etiology of Depression." in Flach, Frederic F., and Draghi, Suzanne C., Eds. *The Nature and Treatment of Depression*. New York: John Wiley and Sons.

Polansky, Norman, et. al. 1981. *Damaged Parents: An Anatomy of Child Neglect*. Chicago: University of Chicago Press.

Prince, Robert. Spring 1985. "Second Generation Effects of Historical Trauma." *The Psychoanalytic Review*. Vol. 72, No. 1, pp. 9-29.

Reid, Jack. 1985. "Adolescent Families: Loosening the Superglue." First Annual Western Conference on Alcoholism and the Family. Anaheim, California. June 9-13.

Rheingold, Joseph C. 1967. *The Mother, Anxiety, and Death: The Catastrophic Death Complex*. Boston: Little, Brown, and Co.

Salzman, Leon. 1975. "Interpersonal Factors in Depression." in Flach, Frederic S., and Draghi, Suzanne C., Eds. *The Nature and Treatment of Depression*. New York: John Wiley and Sons.

Sandler, Joseph. 1960. "On the Concept of the Super Ego," in *The Psychoanalytic Study of the Child*, Vol. 15, New York: International Universities Press.

Sands, Steven. Spring 1985. "Narcissism as a Defense Against Object Loss: Stendhal and Proust." *The Psychoanalytic Review.* Vol. 72, No. 1, pp. 105-127.

Scarf, Maggie. 1980. *Unfinished Business: Pressure Points in the Lives of Women.* New York: Doubleday and Company, Inc.

Shoenberg, Bernard, et. al. 1970. *Loss and Grief: Psychological Management in Medical Practice.* New York: Columbia University Press.

Simos, Bertha. 1976. *A Time to Grieve.* New York: Family Service Association of America.

Szretsky, Ted. 1985. "The Anxiety of Being in Control." *Psychoanalytic Practice.* Adelphi Society for Psychoanalysis and Psychotherapy, Inc. Monograph. pp. 47-55.

Valliant, George. 1983. *The Natural History of Alcoholism.* Cambridge, Mass.: Harvard University Press.

Van Der Kolk, Bessel A., M.D. 1984. "Introduction" in Van Der Kolk, Bessel A., M.D. Ed. *Post-Traumatic Stress Disorder: Psychological and Biological Sequelae.* Washington, D.C.: American Psychiatric Press, Inc.

Van Der Kolk, Bessel A., M.D., and Charles Ducey. 1984. "Clinical Implications of the Rorschach in Post-Traumatic Stress Disorder." in Van Der Kolk, Bessel A., M.D., *Post-Traumatic Stress Disorder: Psychological and Biological Sequelae.* Washington, D.C.: American Psychiatric Press, Inc.

Waelder, R. 1960. *The Basic Theory of Psychoanalysis.* New York: International Universities Press.

Wegscheider-Cruse, Sharon. 1981. *Another Chance.* Palo Alto: Science and Behavior Books.

Wegscheider-Cruse, Sharon. 1985. *Choice Making for Co-Dependents, Adult Children, and Spirituality Seekers.* Pompano Beach, Florida: Health Communications, Inc.

Winnicott, D.W. 1965. *Maturational Processes and the Facilitating Environment: Studies in the Theory of Emotional Development.* New York: International Universities Press.

Woititz, Janet. 1983. *Adult Children of Alcoholics.* Hollywood, Florida: Health Communications, Inc.